# PUERTO RICO: THE GOLDEN YEARS BEFORE IT ALL HIT THE FAN

## (Memoirs of a Raconteur Radio Host)

### Tim Schaefer

*Virgin River Press*

virgriver77@gmail.com

# Table of Contents

Publication details

About the Author

Dedication

| | |
|---|---|
| Foreword | 1 |
| Chapter 1: Good Lovin' | 3 |
| Chapter 2: The Beginning | 5 |
| Chapter 3: Start Me Up | 7 |
| Chapter 4: The Girls | 10 |
| Chapter 5: The Guys | 12 |
| Chapter 6: Intrepid Little Bed | 15 |
| Chapter 7: Shining Star | 19 |
| Chapter 8: Trickle Down Effect | 22 |
| Chapter 9: Dance to the Music | 25 |
| Chapter 10: Opportunity Knocks | 27 |
| Chapter 11: Grand Theft | 28 |
| Chapter 12: A Love Supreme | 31 |
| Chapter 13: Jingle All the Way | 34 |
| Chapter 14: Summer in the City | 37 |
| Chapter 15: Angel of the Morning | 38 |
| Chapter 16: Lady in Red | 41 |
| Chapter 17: Spaced Cowboy | 44 |
| Chapter 18: Up with People, Down with Pants | 48 |
| Chapter 19: Twilight Zone | 50 |

| | |
|---|---|
| Chapter 20: It's All Fun and Games until Someone's Eyes Pop Out | 52 |
| Chapter 21: Girls on the Half Shell | 55 |
| Chapter 22: Saturday Night's Alright for Fightin' | 57 |
| Chapter 23: It's Only a Game, Right? | 62 |
| Chapter 24: Clap for the Wolf Man | 66 |
| Chapter 25: Simon Says | 68 |
| Chapter 26: Beat Me Daddy, Eight to the Bar | 71 |
| Chapter 27: Brain Fart | 73 |
| Chapter 28: Birds Fly in the Fall | 74 |
| Chapter 29: Sock it to Me Baby | 75 |
| Chapter 30: Flashback: I'm In with the Out | 80 |
| Chapter 31: Back to the Future | 82 |
| Chapter 32: The Ugly Truth | 84 |
| Chapter 33: Got Game | 87 |
| Chapter 34: Who Am I? (Ooh Ooh, Ooh Ooh) | 89 |
| Chapter 35: Flashback: School Daze | 91 |
| Chapter 36: Up on the Roof | 92 |
| Chapter 37: Return to Me | 97 |
| Chapter 38: Bob, Ted, Carol and Alice Revisited | 102 |
| Chapter 39: Bus Stop | 107 |
| Chapter 40: Damn Hippies | 110 |
| Chapter 41: Smiling Faces | 113 |
| Chapter 42: Trojan Horse | 120 |
| Chapter 43: Rubber Ball! (Bouncy Bouncy!) | 123 |

Chapter 44: Flashback: It's Fun to Stay at the        131
Chapter 45: Look Sharp, Be Sharp                      134
Chapter 46: Ebony and Ivory                           137
Chapter 47: I Read the News Today, Oh Boy             143
Chapter 48: Beauty and the Beast                      150
Chapter 49: To the Moon, Alice!                       155
Chapter 50: Lotta Freaks!                             157
Chapter 51: The Times They Were a Changin'            162
Chapter 52: Doomsday in Dallas                        164
Chapter 53: Love is All You Need                      166
Chapter 54: They Got Some Crazy Little Women          168
Chapter 55: A Love that Shines                        174
Chapter 56: 1973                                      182
Chapter 57: Radio Rock                                184
Chapter 58: Roll Up for the Mystery Tour              186
Chapter 59: Time Warp in Aisle #5                     188
Chapter 60: Oh, One Last Thing                        190
Acknowledgments                                       191

# Publication details

Cover design by OJ Modjeska

Copyright © 2019 by Tim Schaefer
All rights reserved

ISBN: 978-0-578-56603-0

# About the Author

Tim Schaefer spent way too many years as a rock n roll radio deejay—"town to town, up and down the dial"—yet somehow survived. He resides in the southwestern United States, where he feels right at home with the vermin and the varmints of the desert.

Also by Tim Schaefer

*Darwin's Moon*

*Last Tango In Timbuktu*

*Turn Back Tomorrow*

# Dedication

*For The Wolfman (who cackles on in my heart).*

# Foreword

I was blessed to have lived and loved on the island of Puerto Rico during an idyllic time—a five year span from 1968-1973. Long before all the crap hit the fan. And when the crap hits the fan, there's going to be a major cleanup operation. I am, of course, referring to Hurricane Maria—the lives it claimed, the utter devastation it wrought, and a woefully inadequate response from the U. S. government that remains the subject of much controversy today.

During my tenure on the island, we never had an official hurricane. The average time span between hurricanes is said to be five years. So maybe we just ducked it. Or maybe climate change is sparking more frequent storms of larger intensity now. There is more than a little evidence to support that theory.

The courageous and resilient people of Puerto Rico will continue along the road to recovery. But what I want to do now is take you away from all of that. Back to a magical time, the story of a legendary radio station, and the rollicking times that were had by those of us who were a part of it. It was a wild, exciting time to be young, and I'd be remiss if I didn't present it in all its free-lovin' free-wheeling glory! (Viewer discretion advised: Language. Nudity. Sexual Situations.) It was all about the music, an attitude, and a vision of a new and better world.

This memoir is not "based upon a true story." It IS a true story.

(Aside from public figures, the names and distinguishing characteristics of certain individuals have been changed to protect their anonymity). Everything in these pages actually happened. And that made it a dangerous thing for me to write. And, maybe for you to read. But the sand is running swiftly through the hourglass, and it's time for me to own up and let the chips fall where they may. I've brought some spicy salsa to go along with those chips. Lots of it.

*Buen Provecho!*
—Tim Schaefer

# Chapter 1

## *GOOD LOVIN'*

Goin' down to the *beisbol* stadium
Hiram Bithorn by name
goin' to the Rascals concert
groovin' on a Sunday evening
gotta be there on time
cuz I'm
introducing the group onstage
in all my paisley finery
and sandals

And when my name is announced
a roar goes up
and one of the hippies who is mooching
off me at my pad
said I got bigger applause
than The Rascals—
(not true, but it was close)

And I see
a sea
of adoring young faces
gazing up at me
the hero worship in their eyes
ain't no hero
but I play one on the radio
and I flash them the peace sign
and they flash it right back

Intoxicated
and carried away by the moment
I remove my sandals
and toss them
one by one
into the crowd
and they scramble for those

smelly things
and someone will probably
wear them home tonight

And here they are
ladies and gentlemen
THE RASCALS
as Good Lovin'
fills the warm night air
carried on the breeze
and even the trees
are swaying

This
is as good as it gets
and now I'm just waiting
for someone to come along
And wash my feet

# Chapter 2

## *THE BEGINNING*

It was a brilliant scheme. Five guys and me, calling the same house home. Thirty-five bucks apiece and that paid for a month's rent. It worked for me. I had recently been, uh, relieved of my duties at a local radio station. A couple of us had jobs, but most of my housemates were in similar straits.

Food was scarce. Sometimes we would make a run to the fast food joints—doing this "alms for the poor" thing—and they would donate hard-crusted burgers and sandwiches that otherwise would have ended up in the dumpster. But we had our own place, and we could drink all the booze we wanted (when there was any) and throw parties every night.

The main drawback was that you often had to stand in line at the bathroom door, as if you were waiting to use the lavatory on a plane. Sometimes there was simply no alternative but to pee in the sink.

I thought I was being discreet. No one in the kitchen. I turned off the lights, unzipped, stood on my tiptoes and...the lights flashed on and there stood Johnny—the most obnoxious dude in the house. He shouted, BUSTED, MAN! CAUGHT YA RED HANDED...HEY EVERYBODY, TIMMY'S WANKIN' IT IN THE SINK! Despite my protestations of innocence, he carried on relentlessly. The worst part was that there were girls in the house.

One especially gray, bone-chilling Iowa day—the temperature hovering around zero—the phone rang and one of the guys yelled, "It's for you!"

Someone from Puerto Rico was on the line. I had seen this ad in a broadcasting magazine to the effect of: *New American radio station, owned by Bob Hope, in sunny San Juan, Puerto Rico, now recruiting on-air personnel.* As a lark, I sent them my audition tape and resume. Doesn't hurt to dream, right? Now the station manager was on the phone saying that they liked my tape, and they liked the caption I had put beneath my photo that said, "This is not a mug shot."

The dream was coming true.

The last thing he said was that they would send me a contract in the mail. Gonna work for Bob Hope in the sunny Caribbean! I went outside and breathed in that icicle air and told myself to always remember this moment.

# Chapter 3

## *START ME UP*

January 1968, when I first plunked down on the island, began one of the most tumultuous years in American history. The Vietnam war was raging. Students were raging, pouring into the streets of every major city in protest.

Chicago's Mayor Richard Daley would set his berserko police minions upon the protestors outside the Democratic National Convention to crack some heads open. And crack they did. Martin Luther King Jr. would be assassinated in April (on my goddamned birthday!) and Robert Kennedy would fall just a couple months later. Richard Nixon would be elected president.

In PR we were insulated from the brunt of that turmoil. We got the news reports, of course. But we were a year away from Woodstock, and the peace and love vibe was settling over us like a haze of marijuana smoke, and along with it the proverbial sex, drugs, and rock n roll. I was there to provide the rock n roll. The rest of it would feed off of that.

San Juan was a haven for a small group of U.S. expats who had carved out a niche for themselves. Some were running shops or bars. Others solicited tricks on the streets of the Old City—whatever they had to do. My mission was to become a star, as part of the very first English language Top 40 radio station to hit the island. And we hit like gangbusters. The locals had not previously been exposed to American pop music in such an accessible way, and it was nothing less than a local musical revolution.

But I'm jumping ahead again. Bob Hope's baby, WBMJ 1190, was almost ready to take its first steps. Almost. As a commonwealth of the United States, Puerto Rico's radio and TV stations were regulated by the FCC, that governmental agency that grants you a license and tells you when you are ready to pass go and collect your 200 bucks in funny money. We had expected to hit the airwaves in January, but the start date kept getting put back. There is no rhyme or reason for how or why the FCC determines these things, but General Manager Bob Bennett assured us that we'd be up and running "any day now."

Any day now turned into several months.

And since all of the deejays (henceforth to be referred to as "jocks") were under contract and they couldn't just can our asses, we were paid our full salaries for doing essentially nothing. A lengthy paid vacation in paradise! Uncle Bob wanted us to check in—take the elevator up to our Penthouse studios in the San Juan Darlington hotel—and ask if there was anything to do each day, and the answer would invariably be no. That left us with no choice but to go down to the pool and soak up some rays with a fruity concoction from the pool bar in hand, or head out and explore the beaches.

Two days a week, we would drop in for our employer provided Spanish lessons at Berlitz, where a lovely young Peruvian lady would give us the basics. Ric, Bobby and I (more on them later) learned to put together creative phrases such as: *Yo pongo mi pinga en su boca* (I put my dick in your mouth), and: *No la maleta en mi esposa* (Don't put that briefcase in my wife!). It's all fun and games until your instructor looks over your test results. I believe she thought of us as somewhat charming goof-offs—not terribly serious about learning.

My real education, however, was just ahead.

# Chapter 4

## *THE GIRLS*

A radio acquaintance of mine, who was something of a philosopher, said that you could choose a career path aiming to make you a lot of money, or you could choose one that would likely get you a lot of ass, and that most of the guys in radio had chosen it for the latter. One had to have priorities in life, and he had made me come to grips with mine in just that many words...

Siddhartha (The Buddha) experienced the extremes of hedonism (the path of desire) and asceticism (path of self-denial) on his journey toward enlightenment. It appeared to me that if I was going to follow his example, I'd need to start with one or the other. Which one I chose will become readily apparent.

*

There was never any shortage of tourist chicks. They descended upon the island like Manna from the sky. Most often they would travel in pairs and split expenses, which made for a very doable getaway from New York and anywhere on the east coast.

The best and easiest place to meet them was at a hotel pool. Adjacent outdoor bar essential. They gravitated to the beachside hotels—La Concha, The Flamboyan, The Sheraton—that dotted Ashford Avenue in The Condado, especially in the winter. The pickins' were good in these spots. But you'd be more apt to run into *The Material Girl* there. My home base was the Darlington.

It was a few miles back from the beach, but the prices were more attractive to a certain type of budget-minded traveler—and I dare say, a more down to earth one.

It didn't take long to understand that the ladies were after the same things that drove me on. Physical connection. Maybe a little tenderness if it happened to be included in the bargain. There were many who weren't averse to winging their way down and falling hard for a guy in that dream tropical setting, and continuing the relationship—at least by correspondence—when they got back home.

The girls were loosey-goosey. But one of them set me straight about that. She said that she would never do the kinds of things back home in Buffalo that she'd been doing here on the island. She had a reputation to protect! (Remember, we were still in the day when that seemed to count for something with young women, before the influence of Madonna, Miley, et al.) She had revealed to me—and it was my first big epiphany about women—that the only difference between a nice girl and a slut were those three little words: *Location. Location. Location.*

# Chapter 5

## *THE GUYS*

Those days and months waiting for our time to shine went by slowly. We were chomping at the bit. Ric Roberts, Bobby West, General Manager Bob Bennett, Program Director Bill Thompson, and myself would ostensibly comprise WBMJ's initial on-air lineup. Oh, and I was *Charlie Brown*. When Bob Bennett was tossing out potential air names for me to yea or nay, it seemed to fit.

Ric was impish, with a wry wit, and was something of a kindred spirit, I felt. He was a born performer, and later that year would star in a local San Juan production of *Guys And Dolls*, surprising the hell out of not only me, but everyone else with his singing and dancing ability.

Bobby was a tall, cool drink of water who looked like a young Clint Eastwood. He wore his dark wrap-around shades indoors and out. He seemed the most anxious of the guys to get on with our purpose for being here, and the most frustrated. In the end, the enchantment of Puerto Rico alone was not enough to keep him hanging on. He decided to return to the states.

Bobby was replaced by Johnny Ringo. He was a former Marine, and if ever there were a personality totally opposite to mine, he was it. He had chosen a cowboy name for his moniker because, essentially, he was John Wayne. And he wasn't exactly enthralled with folks who weren't square-jawed and Caucasian like himself.

The on-air barbs flew fast and furious between Ringo and myself. Listeners thought we were feuding, but it was just show business. We were entertainers first and foremost, and we'd all taken a page out of Don Rickles' playbook. It was like one continuous roast back and forth. As long as the other guy mentioned your name, you didn't care what he said. You'd pay him back when your shift came around.

Bob Bennett and others on his management staff were of the gay persuasion. No big deal. Except that back then it actually was. And while San Juan was known as something of a haven for gay folk at the time, you didn't just come out and flaunt it, especially if you held a position in the public eye. There was still too much prejudice at the time. And of course, there was the Catholic church.

One night early on, a couple weeks after my arrival, Bennett invited me to his place for dinner. It was a cozy and well-appointed apartment in the old city. He made some Italian dish, and we had some wine. He was a friendly and convivial boss.

After dinner, we carried our *vino* and our conversation out onto his second floor balcony. We were sitting and sipping for a while, observing the street scene below, when he rose abruptly and switched off all the lights in the place—leaving us in pitch black darkness. I had to make my own interpretation of where things were leading, and I indicated that I thought it was time to go. He was disappointed, but I think it's what saved my job in the long run. Had I been a switch hitter and allowed things to progress, he could have just used me for a while and thrown me away. This way I had established my boundaries. He respected them and he never hit on me again.

# Chapter 6

## *INTREPID LITTLE BED*

She wasn't a hooker. Not exactly. About twenty. Petite. Panamanian. With a worldly air that belied her age. Yes, she approached me on the street, but all she seemed to want was a place to crash. What the hell. I had room, and always willing to rescue a fair, or dusky, damsel in distress.

There was room, yes, but very little of it on the rollaway—the only piece of furniture in my place—loaned to me at that by a landlady who'd correctly pegged me as newly arrived and traveling light.

It was an attractive apartment though, there in *Viejo San Juan*—and the neighbors! I was next door to the Puerto Rican governor's mansion, *La Fortaleza*, and directly across the street from famed cellist Pablo Casals. I never actually saw the reclusive genius, nor did the governor see fit to invite me over for tea, but it made for some good name dropping nonetheless.

In the mornings I'd wake to gentle sunlight streaming through the shutters, and the tickling sensation of tiny lizards thrashing about in my hair. Tourists would stroll past and comment on what they could see of my little abode from the outside.

"Governor's staff residence, most likely," I'd hear them say.

What if they knew that inside on a musty smelling rollaway

sat a burping, scratching, hung-over young gringo in his skivvies—smirking at the irony of it all?

Her name was Tina. She knew my name, but preferred to call me *Stupido*. I took it as a term of endearment.

She stayed over. I'd leave in the mornings, and she'd head off to God knows where. In the evenings, she'd return. It was a tight fit, the two of us on a bed built for one. Tight but cozy.

One night she showed up with a friend. A rather rotund American chick named Rosie. The connection between the two of them was unclear. Rosie needed a place "just for the night." I said okay, but as you can see, you'll have to crash on the floor. No problem, she said. No, I don't mind at all.

We settled in for the night. Rosie seemed content, sacked out in the corner. I had no mat, or even a blanket to lend her. She was fortunate, though, in that the meat on her bones would serve as a buffer.

The floor is hard. The pavement is harder.

In the dream, I was being smothered...crushed underneath some formless, nameless weight. I woke with a start. The nightmare was real. Rosie had clambered onto the bed, AND sprawled across the two of us like a giant tortoise that's discovered the ideal nesting spot. What's more, she was out cold. The tiny bed strained under its burden. Somehow, I managed to slide from beneath the intruding beast and tumble to the floor.

"*Stupido*, what's going on?"

I didn't bother to explain. It was three o'clock in the morning and to say that I was annoyed would be an understatement. I grabbed Rosie by her shirt and literally dragged her off the bed, depositing her as gently as I could (under the circumstances) back onto the floor.

In the morning, she was apologetic. "I don't know what got into me," she said...

"That's okay," I replied, beginning to feel like a heartless bastard. That is, until I considered the alternatives: Tina and Rosie in the bed...me on the floor. Unacceptable. Tina on the floor...me and the tortoise on the bed.

*Totally* unacceptable.

"I'll be good tonight," said Rosie.

In the evening, we resumed our rightful places. Tina and me on the rollaway. Rosie the obedient dog on the floor. All was right with the world.

1am. Rosie was sprawled across us on the bed.

I got up, grabbed her by the arms, and pulled. She offered no resistance, nor did she move of her own volition. She was simply dead weight that needed to be transported from one location to another. I dragged her off the bed and deposited her back onto the floor.

"STAY! STAY DOWN," I scolded.

4am. The tortoise was *baaaacck!* I grabbed hold of her legs, ready to give her the old heave-ho. But now she was desperate, clinging to the side of the bed with all her might. I pulled. She tightened her grip. It was an epic battle, but Rosie's ass finally went THUMP as it hit the floor.

In the morning, I delivered Tina's dose of reality. Rosie had to go.

That evening I slipped the key into the slot and poked my head cautiously inside the door. A dead calm. They were both gone. Cleared out. Not a trace of them, save for a noticeable sag in the middle of my intrepid little bed.

A couple days later, I spotted Tina hanging out on the street corner. She didn't look my way.

Yeah, I guess maybe she was a hooker.

# Chapter 7

## *SHINING STAR*

On May 9th, 1968, WBMJ cranked it up and began broadcasting its unique sound to Puerto Rico and all of the Caribbean—and, according to some of the mail we received, they were picking us up loud and clear as far away as Sweden and Norway. Keep them cards and letters comin' in!

Our only English language competition was WHOA 870. They featured a middle-of-the-road type format that catered to "grown-ups," so they were no real competition for the younger demographic that we'd be scooping up when we started rocking the island.

A sidelight here. A young woman named Sally Jessy was beginning her radio broadcasting career at WHOA, doing the 6 to 9 a.m. shift with "comedy, weather, and news." You'll remember her as noted television talk show host Sally Jessy Raphael. But all that came much later. (More on Sally—and something I did that got me on her shit list—a little further on, dear reader!)

I had started out on the mid-day shift, where we were playing pretty much a straight Top 40 type format. But Bob Bennett, in his infinite wisdom, saw me as more of a creature of the night. He was going to open things up after 7pm. Throw in some album cuts, even progressive stuff like Iron Butterfly and King Crimson. I would soon be laying "21st Century Schizoid Man" on them, and that was gonna blow their already weed-addled minds! I didn't have to think long about making the switch. The daylight hours were regarded as prime time for radio (the opposite of television), but I was intending to turn that thinking upside down by developing a loyal cult following of denizens of the night when our signal went skipping across the Atlantic to Europe and beyond. Night time was gonna be the right time for Charlie Brown.

*

It was the debut of my new after dark presence, and Uncle Bob wanted me to kick it off with "Jumpin' Jack Flash" by The Stones because it was number one on the charts. Bennett was a veteran of stateside Top 40 radio, and he liked to do things by the book. So kicking off my show with the number one song made sense to him. But I had a little more imagination. I wanted to bust out of the gate with a song that would be an anthem for my generation, and make a defining statement about what listeners could expect from my show. And I had just the right one picked out. But nobody's heard of that record...or the group for that matter, Bennett said. But the song just works, I told him. And it's gonna be a hit—a huge one! I can feel it and I can do my little part in making that come about right here tonight.

    We argued our points back and forth. What the hell did he care what I opened with 'cept he wanted to be in control? I could see the longer this would go the better chance he'd have of winning out.

    But...

Finally he shrugged and gave in, and I hit the ground running at seven with Steppenwolf's soon to be classic: *BORN TO BE WI-EEE-ILLLD!!!*

*DNNN DU DU DU DNNN DU DU DU*
*BORN TO BE WI-EEE-ILLLD!!!*

# Chapter 8

## *TRICKLE DOWN EFFECT*

Shortly after our launch, Bob Bennett engineered a lavish bash to welcome the public and promote the station at the swankiest hotel on the island, *El San Juan*. There were gigantic portraits of all the jocks draping the walls of the dining area. I was reminded of the song where the man with the big cigar says, "C'mere boy—I'm gonna make you a star!"

I was camped out on the second floor mezzanine, surveying the party goers below. A mother in her early forties and her seventeen year-old daughter had glommed onto me. The daughter—decked out in a white taffeta gown—parked herself on my knee. I was hoping to get an opening to discreetly ask her when her next birthday would be rolling around. Mom, who was quite well preserved for what I thought of as old—about twenty years my senior—was amiable and unconcerned.

The three of us were getting sloshed, and that wasn't a good thing for me to do in mixed company. Or any company. I looked down and saw a young couple at a table directly below us. I was nursing a gin and tonic, and decided to have a little fun. I leaned over the railing and begin to dribble my drink onto the top of the man's head. He jerked around and looked up, obviously pissed. I gave a little wave and ducked back out of his line of vision, hoping he wouldn't compare me with my portrait on the wall and put two and two together. Wouldn't make the best first impression. Mom and daughter were yukking it up.

A couple days hence, the "old" lady and I ended up tangled together amongst the sheets. She knew exactly what she was doing, using her offspring as bait to reel me in.

Ah, the wisdom of age.

*

It was unexpected, but early on it became clear that I was going to be the Top-Of-The-Christmas-Tree-Shining-Star of the station. That's not to take anything away from the other guys. They were all witty and talented, but I had tapped into something with our audience—endeared myself to them in some almost mystical kind of way. Maybe it was just that I was a hoot to listen to when people were stoned. I presented this frenetic, wacky persona. I'd go into this black hipster thing—deepening my voice and giving it a slight southern twang. Then out of sheer exuberance, my voice would skew into a falsetto register with *IT'S BOOGIE BLAST-OFF TIME*—shouting it over that wild majestic organ intro to "Gimme Some Lovin" by The Spencer Davis Group.

I coined the phrase: *synchronize your belly buttons!* Like, I'd do a time check and say, "It's 10:21 at the new WBMJ...synchronize your belly buttons!" It was just a nonsensical thing to get people to scratch their heads and smile. Then the more I thought about it, I realized it had a sexual connotation. If two people's belly buttons were in synch with one another, what they'd be doing would be obvious. I started using the phrase more often after that.

Many of the listeners thought I was black. I wasn't mocking. I was channeling. I had grown up with the Amos and Andy TV show, and I loved those guys. Wolfman Jack had been my late night bedside companion. And there was this batshit crazy guy out of Chicago—Dick Biondi—who sounded like Jerry Lewis hopped up on amphetamines. They were all my early influences. But Charlie Brown was my own unique creation.

# Chapter 9

## *DANCE TO THE MUSIC*

I heard the rap on my door. I opened it and there was Alba, one of the dark-haired, dark-eyed local chicks who, a few nights earlier, had ridden me on an office chair up at Penthouse One. She'd gazed deep into my eyes with a sick twisted sneer on her lips. There was twenty years of repressed Catholic schoolgirl sexuality coming forth in a tidal wave and I let it wash over me. I guess she was into it.

"Hurry up, Charlie," she said. "Everyone's waiting for you!"

I was still in my swim trunks and she had noticed that my member was starting to wake up inside there in her honor. She traced the outline of it with her fingertips.

"Okay...okay," I said, knowing that we'd better put anything off for now. "I'll be down as soon as I change." A local high school was holding a dance in *my honor* down at the ballroom of the Darlington! I was stunned. When I walked in there the place was packed and a band was beating out a rock rhythm. I needed to get up in front of them and say something. I stepped up to a mic and flashed the peace sign, and a sea of adoring young faces beamed back at me. I thanked them profusely. They presented me with a plaque, for God's sake! It said: *Charlie Brown—Disc-Jockey Of The Year*. Or that's what it was supposed to say. But whoever engraved it wrote jocker instead of jockey. Didn't matter.

That endeared it to me all the more. I was a jockey...a jocker...a joker. I was two weeks into my new night time gig.

It was going to be a wild ride.

# Chapter 10

## *OPPORTUNITY KNOCKS*

The truth is, it wasn't easy for me to approach women. I had been a shy kid in school, and I didn't take rejection well. It *hurt*, goddamnit! I wasn't going to just walk up to a nubile lass and try to sell myself. I was more of an opportunist—waiting for an opening where I could enter the picture nonchalantly (or seemingly so).

If I saw one of my friends chatting up a chick, I'd move in on him. Maybe stand close to the two of them pretending to be interested in their conversation. Eventually my friend would have to acknowledge my presence and introduce me. Then if I spotted her alone later on, I'd feel comfortable in going over and starting my own chat with her.

In the animal kingdom it's called *kleptoparasitism*. One animal stealing the prey that was caught by another animal. *The kleptoparasite gains prey or objects not otherwise attainable or which otherwise require time and effort. However, the kleptoparasite might be injured by the victim in cases in which the latter defends its prey* (Wikipedia).

I was willing to take my chances on that score.

# Chapter 11

## GRAND THEFT

The roof garden adjacent to our studios gave a panoramic view of the shimmering lights of San Juan at night. Daytime it was a good spot to observe the hotel pool and check out the action.

Oh...what's this??? I spotted Ric chatting up a girl relaxing on a chaise. My animal instincts kicked in and I was in that elevator and going down...going down... lickety-split. I strolled casually up to the two of them like hey, I'm *another* of those fascinating radio guys you're just going to love to meet! Ric took it in stride, like he was expecting some of the other vultures to already start picking up the scent.

Her name was Allison. She was down for the week from upstate New York and would be staying two more days. It was me on one side of her and Ric on the other like a couple of stereo speakers. She heard the bass and looked over at him. She heard the drums and looked over at me.

Ric had to be somewhere. Too bad. I lingered with Ally for another half hour, shooting the tropical breeze. Next day I saw her solo at the pool and I moved in. She had this worldly look about her, though she was all of twenty-four. She sent out a vibe that said if you play your cards right, you could get lucky.

I got lucky, and was invited up to her room that evening. We were making out on her bed and I thought things were going my way. But then she stopped and said she didn't want to do it with me.

"Uh...why not?"

"Because you're a nice guy."

Oh Jesus, here it comes. I won't go into the complex machinations of the female brain that causes many of them to reason that if you are "nice" you don't deserve to get laid. It was just my job to convince her otherwise. (You could say the whole point of this writing exercise is to help me figure out if I was indeed a nice guy...or a bastard. Perhaps by the final chapter I'll have a handle on it.)

"I'm not really that nice, I said."

"Yeah...you are…"

"No, I'm not...I'm a bastard when you really get to know me."

She chuckled. "I don't believe you."

"Look at me...I'm such a bastard!"

"Uh...I don't know…"

"Bastard to the core!"

"Hmmm…"

I don't know how many times I said *bastard* (and I think I also threw asshole in there a few times for good measure). Until I saw something primal...something reverting back to the dawn of human history register in her brain: *Ugh...he bastard...bastard make good mate...*

And with that the panties came off...and I was IN!

Afterward, we crashed out and the morning light found us there together.

I learned that she had spent much of the previous evening with Ric. Now I see what her reluctance with me was about. Though she didn't come right out and say that she had done the nasty with him, I assumed it to be so. She was thinking: should I do two different guys on successive nights? Then the realization that she was in the *Caribbean* with no reputation to protect, so what the hell.

Early in the morning there came a discreet rap upon the door. It was Ric, obviously looking to hit it one more time. The awkward look of surprise on his face when he saw me there...well, it was *precious*. We exchanged a few pleasantries and then he took off.

Bottom line, I didn't feel sorry for the man. His wife was waiting for him at home.

# Chapter 12

## *A LOVE SUPREME*

Ric, Johnny, and I had been granted an informal interview session with the world's number one female singing group. So there I was, knocking on their hotel room door—expecting some big flunky whose sole purpose was to run interference to be standing there. But it was Diana herself who answered. She was wearing pedal pushers and her hair was frizzed out—so much for the glamor girl image. I was struck by how thin she was.

"Hi, come on in," she said.

Mary and Cindy were there, hanging out. Berry Gordy Junior's mother—a large, convivial woman—was there too. And, oh yeah, a couple of crashers—two moon-eyed young lesbians who were casual acquaintances of mine. Nobody seemed to know how or why they were there, except that they seemed to pop up with uncanny regularity wherever I went.

I sat at one end of the sofa. There was a narrow space between the couch and the overstuffed chair that was next to it. Diana squeezed through the opening and her butt cheek rubbed right up against my shoulder as she glided by! She didn't say excuse me. She must instinctively have known that I wouldn't mind. And while I figured that my "brush" with greatness was unintentional on her part, I vowed that someday I would put it in a tell-all memoir of some kind.

Johnny and Ric had the presence of mind to ask a couple of music related questions, while I sat in a daze, still giddy over what had just occurred. Berry Gordy Junior's mom took over the conversation, talking about her son, the architect of the Motown Sound. She told a story about The Temptations, but the only thing that registered in my mind were the words, *Temptin' Temptations*, which she would repeat at intervals like a litany. The moon-eyed girls were beaming, soaking it all in and holding onto one another.

Mary, who struck me as the cutest of the three (and more my type), mentioned something about being from Chicago. Later, sensing an opening, I approached her and said something stupid about having once lived there myself, and wasn't that a coincidence! She had grasped my outstretched hand, holding onto it longer than what would be merely polite...much longer, in fact, and suddenly I was moonstruck.

When the party broke up, some of us milled around in the hallway. One of the crasher chicks, noticing that she had made off with a hotel drinking glass, collared Cindy as she walked by, shoved the glass at her and said, "Hey, would you take this back to the room for me?"

Cindy stared down at the glass, and I could see the wheels of her mind turning, as if to say: *We marched on Selma, braved police dogs and fire hoses, stood up to Governor Wallace in the doorway of that schoolhouse...for THIS?*

She sat the glass in a spittoon next to the elevator and walked away.

Back home in my apartment, I fell into a blue funk for the better part of a week, thinking about Mary—what could and could never be—and coming to grips with what a pathetically lonely asshole I was.

Hopelessly infatuated with a Supreme.

# Chapter 13

## *JINGLE ALL THE WAY*

We had the PAMS jingle package. The gold standard. In both English and Spanish. They were *swingin'*. We had all the bells and whistles. Literally. There was a button that generated a "beep" tone that we had to press after every song before opening our mouths. We had 20/20 news. While everybody else ran their news at the top of the hour, we ran it at twenty past and twenty to. It was a gimmick. Within the news itself, there was another button you pressed to generate a staccato burst of high-pitched electronic beeps that served as an attention getter between news stories. There was a reverb that gave our voices more of a presence than what you would hear on the other radio stations. It was nuts, but it was Bob Bennett's thing. The one thing all the carnival sounds accomplished was that there was never any doubt about what station you were listening to.

There was this thing I did at night called "Make It Or Break It". We were always getting new music in, a lot of it, often by relatively unknown artists. I'd audition some of the songs before the show, and if I found something good, or pretty bad, it would be the Make It Or Break It song for that night. I'd play the record and listeners would vote on it. The votes would determine if we added the song to our playlist, or if I would physically destroy the record on the air. If a song was voted down, I'd hold the record up to the microphone and let them hear me cracking it into little pieces. Except if it was a song I personally liked, I'd substitute some shitty 45 to break instead and keep the good song for myself.

"Scramble Tunes" had snippets of five different songs spliced together, and a listener calling in would have to correctly identify all five songs to win eleven dollars and ninety cents (big money!). The sound bites were no more than a second or two in length, and almost nobody ever won, except once in a while we'd make it a little easier to get a winner. I recorded this little gremlin voice that said: *AHA, YOU LOSE!* And then a chorus in the background would go *awwww* (so sad). I'd say, "Well, there goes another loser on the Charlie Brown show!" It was mischievous, but they ate it up.

A listener called me one night and said, "I almost drove off a bridge because I was laughing so hard!" That's always gratifying to hear, but I didn't want to be responsible for someone crashing through a guardrail and doing a Mary Jo Kopechne on me in the drink.

The best promotion—from my standpoint at least—was the Slave For A Day Contest. Listeners would write in and say why they wanted Charlie Brown to be their slave for a day, and what kind of stuff they would make me do. (If I had been black, this wouldn't have been a great idea). Their wish would be my command. This, of course, opened it up to all sorts of recklessness and debauchery—and some of the females (and some of the men) were not coy about their intentions. The best part of it was I got to pick the winner. I know you're thinking that I would just choose the person who seemed most likely to hop into the sack with me. I'll have to admit that was my intention in the beginning, but at the last minute my conscience got the better of me and I actually picked the entry I thought was the most deserving in terms of creativity and cleverness.

It turned out to be a little dark mocha gal named Luisa, who came up to the station to meet me. Within half an hour her hand was down inside my jeans. Luisa began visiting my apartment on a regular basis after that, and a good time was had by all. Moral of the story: when you do the right thing and cast your selfish desires aside, sometimes the universe gives you a pat on the back and says *good boy*—now go and get your rocks off anyway!

# Chapter 14

## *SUMMER IN THE CITY*

I thought a lot about Ally after she returned home. There was something about her to be sure. She was hip. She had a sense of humor. And she was something of a whore. It's the whore part I found most intriguing. That's biblical, after all, and little did I know that I was on the verge of undergoing my own "death and resurrection."

I sensed there could be more between us than just the one night stand. I knew she was in school in upstate New York, and that her summer break was coming up soon. I wrote her a letter. A lot of pen-pal type crap until the last few lines. And then I said: *Would you like to come down and live with me for the summer?*

I had no idea what her reaction might be. But I sent it off with the same doesn't-hurt-to-dream gleam in my eye that was there on that winter day when I sent my audition tape off to—of all places—Puerto Rico.

# Chapter 15

## *ANGEL OF THE MORNING*

His name was Angelo and he had recently taken over the midnight to six slot. *En la madrugada!* He was a San Juan native (the rest of us were imports) and he looked kind of like Danny Trejo without the rough edges. My show segued into his and I would sometimes hang out to groove and chat with him for a while.

On this particular night a friend of his—I'll call him Carlos—was there and he had taken a small pill bottle out of his pocket.

"What have we here?" I queried.

"It's LSD," said Carlos with no hesitation.

I'd smoked plenty of weed up to that point, but was still a virgin with the psychedelics.

"Wow, I've always wanted to try that."

Carlos glanced at Angelo and said, "Ahh...I don't think he's ready."

Angelo looked at me and said, "Yeah...he's ready."

I, of course, had no idea of what I was getting myself into, but I was willing to put myself out there.

"Just give him a little sliver," Angelo said.

Carlos broke off a bitty piece of one of the pills. It was white flecked with little blue dots. LSD-25. The most potent of the psychotropic substances (as I was about to find out).

I downed it and just hung there, getting into Angelo's selection of tunes. For a while—maybe twenty minutes—I thought there might be no effect. And then I had an overwhelming urge to be alone.

Later, Carlos found me sitting in one of the darkened office rooms, staring into the black void. All my assumptions about who and what I was were sloughing off of me like dead skin, and I needed a quiet place to come to grips with that.

My mind was being blown! My consciousness was expanding. I was connecting with the pure essence of being. The be-all-that-you-can-be. The all-that-you-are, which was the total universe, and I was it and it was me and always had been and always would be forever and ever amen.

Imagine if *all* of that somehow got sucked up and imploded—ZAP—into this tiny vial. Your physical body. And there it sits trapped for the duration. Genie in a bottle. Psychedelics were the just-add-water step that expanded you back into the omniscient cosmic soup of being.

A short way of saying it would be ego death.

I floated back into the control room where Angelo was playing the perfect tripping song, "Mechanical World" by Spirit, with its lyric: *Somebody tell my father that I died.* Randy California's velvet guitar solos speaking to me in a way they never could have before, as the shimmering molecules of pure energy danced before my eyes.

I must have gotten Angelo to play that song a half dozen more times as the night wore on. It seemed to never end. It was a good thing Uncle Bob was zonked out at home or he would have suspected a gang of freaks had commandeered the station (which, in fact, they had!).

Angelo (and if you haven't connected the dots yet, Angelo means "Angel" in Spanish) drove me home at the end of his shift as the dawn was breaking. I remembered him saying earlier: *Death means nothing to me...it's just a transition.* He got me safely tucked inside my apartment. We stood there for a moment and I said, "I-I feel holy. I saw God." He just smiled.

That night, an Angel got his wings.

\*

A few days later I got a letter back from Ally. SHE SAID YES! I was ecstatic. All the flowers were blooming, I had seen God, and Ally was coming down to share my bed with me for the summer. All in all, not a bad week, I thought.

# Chapter 16

## *LADY IN RED*

I picked Ally up at the airport and we caught a cab back to my place. I had recently purchased a little Harley Rapido model bike that I had lots of fun tooling around San Juan on, but I wasn't going to make her mount it first thing out of the gate.

I had moved into the Hotel San Cristobal, a rustic (more like crumbling) old inn on the Boulevard Del Valle overlooking the ocean in *Viejo San Juan*—just a stone's throw from the infamous *La Perla* slum, sitting down there adjacent the beach like a half-eaten mango rotting in the sun. (All I knew about *La Perla* was that you didn't go down there if you valued your life and your personal possessions.)

It was a spacious second story apartment—quite a find for the money—and the sea breeze wafting through my open windows was all we needed to keep our cool. I had a life-size poster of Brigitte Bardot on one wall, and one of black power activist Stokely Carmichael adorning another spot where it was covering up a stain.

Ally loved the place, as did I. The only drawback was that there was a troupe of flamenco dancers occupying the quarters directly above me, and every morning around seven they would practice their routine, with the sharp vocalizations and heels pounding the floor, making my ceiling shake. Neighbors who wanted to sleep in would be yelling, SHUT UP GODDAMNIT!...*PENDEJO!...MARICON!...* and similar epithets in both English and Spanish. All to no avail.

There was a little Italian dining establishment called The Roman Table that was below ground level right beneath the hotel. It had checkerboard tablecloths and atmosphere out the wazoo. Ally and I liked to drop in there to drink wine and eat spaghetti, and when she had a buzz on she would call me "Ducky."

The Roman Table was run by a couple of older queens—really sweet guys—who rolled out the red carpet for us. They knew Bob Bennett and they quickly picked up on who Ally and I were. We had everything at our fingertips. We didn't have to leave the hotel if we didn't care to—we could just stay inside rutting for days at a time in our breezy abode like John and Yoko.

But there would be appearances we would need to make.

*

Ally made her official San Juan public debut, as it were, at the opening night of Guys and Dolls at The Tapia Theater, where Ric Roberts would wow us with his singing, dancing, and acting talent.

Ally had the ability (as do many women) to look totally striking or rather plain, depending on how she was dressed and if she used a touch of makeup. On this night she was a *knockout*. She had asked me what she should wear, and I said just put on something sexy. She took that and ran with it, coming up with a red dress that was so low cut in front that if her twins had been babies in a cradle, I'd have feared they were going to fall out at any moment. (Ally had great boobs...*not too beeg, not too leetle*... as my old man would have said.)

We had front row seats at the theater, and at the end the buzz among the cast was not about the performance...it was about *Ally!* She was hard to miss, and had been a distraction to at least some of the cast members. Ric later told me that one of them had exclaimed: *Who was the TITS in the front row???* I loved that Ally had put herself out there, so to speak. I liked to think of her as a whore. It turned me on.

In that regard, she would not disappoint.

# Chapter 17

## *SPACED COWBOY*

It was easy to pinpoint when The Beatles dropped acid because their music started to reflect it, beginning with the *Revolver* album in 1966. (The dead giveaway was the song "Tomorrow Never Knows." Still one of my favorites.)

Then, notably, came *Sergeant Pepper's Lonely Hearts Club Band* and the *White Album*. Their music became the soundtrack to the kaleidoscopic movie of our lives.

Conversely, it wasn't hard to home in on when Charlie Brown had gone tumbling down his own private rabbit hole. I started regularly playing stuff like:

"Eight Miles High" by the Byrds

Frank Zappa's "Freak Out"

"Soul Experience"—Iron Butterfly

"Purple Haze"—Jimi Hendrix

"I Had Too Much To Dream Last Night"—Electric Prunes

"Spirit In The Sky"—Norman Greenbaum

"Saving Grace—Steve Miller

And let's not forget "Boobs A Lot" by The Fugs. (Did I really play that? It wasn't a psychedelic song except in the sense that somebody had to be high when they wrote it.)

I would sometimes trip while I was doing my show. The good thing about being a loopy kind of air personality was that I don't think listeners could tell the difference one way or the other.

When I finished up at midnight, I would occasionally crash out at the station, with Angel at the helm in the control room. I'd pass out on the floor in the hallway (it was carpeted) and Johnny Ringo and the office staff would find me there when they arrived in the morning. They just stepped over me and went about their business! This is how it is when you've been tagged as the station's "hippie eccentric," too beloved (at least by the listeners) for anyone to give you any shit about it.

Meanwhile, WBMJ was becoming the hottest station this side of Fidel Castro. More important to the music industry was the impact we were having on product sales:

*Tom McGinnis of Columbia records, now headquartered in New York, attributes the station to a complete flip-flop in record sales...*

*—Billboard Magazine*

There was a fellow radio professional, Norm Russell, who was working at WSTX-970 in Saint Croix (U.S. Virgin Islands). He was a big fan of WBMJ. Norm was a pilot, and one day he flew his Piper Cherokee 140 from St. Croix to San Juan to visit me at the radio station. One always paints a mental picture of people they hear on the radio, and it could have been that Norm wasn't exactly picturing Charlie Brown with long blonde hair and and jeans with holes in them! In an online tribute, Russell would later write of WBMJ: "...we could get it very clearly on St. Croix.

Back in the day...it was the hottest station on earth!"

*

Uncle Bob came up with this brilliant idea. He didn't want our listeners to be deprived of their Charlie Brown fix for even one day. I was already on six days a week, but he wanted me to do a segment that would run on Sundays too. Just a couple hours and I could tape the show beforehand, so I would still have my Sundays off. (The generosity of this man astounded me!)

I agreed to do it but it was a pain in the ass. The only good time to record the show was after my night time gig. That meant I'd be in the production room at midnight, pooped and dragged out from the five previous hours of cavorting and snorting I'd already done live. The first couple times I taped the Sunday segment I played it straight. The next week I decided I'd drop some acid right before taping the show, to see how that went. As I was putting on my first record that shit kicked in bigtime, and I started laughing my ass off, because that is what you do when you've been let in on the Cosmic Joke. I taped the entire segment and thought I'd gotten through it okay. Except for when the needle started skipping on a couple of records. *Skipping...and skipping...and skipping.* In my altered state of consciousness I didn't see anything wrong with that (keepin' it real man), so instead of rewinding the tape and taking that out of there, I left it in. My banter was even goofier than what I would normally put out there, to the point of where I knew people had to be scratching their heads.

Uncle Bob was listening on Sunday, and I could just imagine his face when he heard that broken record sound going on for what seemed like a record breaking time.

The next week I taped a similarly WTF kind of show. I was sending a message. If he was going to make me do this, he would have to take whatever he got from his overworked and bedraggled star. On Monday he ducked in just as I was about to go live again and said with a grimace, "Okay, you win. Forget about the Sunday show."

It was an important victory because this is what typically happens in work situations when you're good at what you do—they pile more work on top of you. And usually without a corresponding increase in pay. Don't put up with it.

Just drop some acid and say fuck it.

# Chapter 18

## *UP WITH PEOPLE, DOWN WITH PANTS*

After Ally arrived, of course, I needed to be on my best behavior. Or at least make the effort. No more crashing at the station overnight. And the young hotties, of which there would be a steady stream in and out of Penthouse One, I had to leave alone.

There were a few minor indiscretions.

One day these four sweet Puerto Rican chicks—they were all friends or maybe sisters—came in and hung out for a while. When they were ready to leave, they lined up and wanted me to give each of them a deep soul kiss. I had to oblige. Public relations, you know.

Then there was Jaymie, who ran a women's clothing boutique in the Condado. High fashion type. The only thing she ever wanted was for me to give her oral. She didn't want to reciprocate or take care of me in any fashion. I didn't mind. I was just happy to see her enjoying herself. Score one for the nice guy, right?

One night Jaymie came up to the station while I was on the air and immediately removed her pants. (I was supposed to keep the doors locked after 7pm on Uncle Bob's directive. No visitors. I ignored that, of course.) So Jaymie was prancing around the halls, bottomless (but wearing a fashionable top) waiting for me to service her if I would put on a long record. She knew I was good at multi-tasking.

Then I saw the glass door at the end of the corridor opening up, and there was Johnny Ringo, who had let himself in with his key. Jaymie went into a panic, scrambling to find her pants (where *did* she leave them?). Ringo immediately sensed that something was going on that he shouldn't ask too many questions about. Jaymie emerged after a minute, red-faced but dressed, and greeted the morning man with a sheepish grin.

It wasn't cheating. I did not have sex with that woman! (The definitive word on where you draw the line, as you know, would be established by one of our future presidents.)

# Chapter 19

## *TWILIGHT ZONE*

A lot of folks would show up unexpectedly in Penthouse One, as a matter of fact, and at times it would stretch the bounds of serendipity beyond all believability.

1969 was turning to golden autumn. (In many places...here, it was just lush tropical green). I had just gotten the new Led Zeppelin II album in, and was anxious to debut it for my listeners. I set the needle down on "Ramble On," written by Robert Plant—a good rockin' number that I felt represented the album well.

I looked up and three people were entering my control room. One of them I knew—this comely lass named Stacy who would pop up now and then just like a lot of them. The other two looked *vaguely* familiar. The blonde-tressed freaky looking guy said, "How do you like the album?" Just casual like.

"Great," I said. "I think this is my favorite cut."

"Yeah," he said. "I think it's mine too."

I still wasn't catching on. And then it hit me. This was fucking Robert Plant!!! The drummer, John Bonham, was right on his heels. Here was one half of Led Zeppelin mysteriously entering my control room one minute into the first song I had ever played off their album...in *Puerto Rico*, no less!

Bonham was subdued. Quiet. Plant was animated. He spotted the hundred or so record albums I had scattered about the floor behind me, and he dove into them like a kid on Christmas morning. I had all kinds of stuff down there, but he was getting off on some of the old blues guys: John Lee Hooker...Muddy Waters...Jimmy Reed.

Stacy, of course, was beaming. She had scored a major groupie coup—plucking the two of them off the street somewhere in the Condado as they were strolling about, checking out the city. She'd loaded her prize catches into her car—all too willing to play tour guide—and the three of them cruised, listening to the radio. (WBMJ, natch!)

When Charlie Brown came on, she said, "I know that guy!"

They said, "Take us to that station!"

Led Zeppelin had recently completed their third North American tour. As for the rest of it, and how this woo-woo level of "coincidence" could have occurred...consult with my friend Rod Serling. In *THE TWILIGHT ZONE!*

# Chapter 20

## IT'S ALL FUN AND GAMES UNTIL SOMEONE'S EYES POP OUT

Ally began to endear herself to the WBMJ staff. Uncle Bob liked her. Or at least respected her as someone who might be able to keep me in line, to some extent. Meanwhile, I was doing my part to encourage Ally to get out of line. We were all about the twisted laughs, and that was true of everybody in the place. There were times when we *might* have carried it too far.

One of the news guys—Neal—was a fresh-faced, just out of college type, and we liked to screw with him while he was delivering his sober news stories. Ally went in and took a lighter out of her purse and set fire to one edge of the news copy Neal was holding in his hand. He gesticulated wildly, flailing at the flame while trying not to lose his "authoritative" newsman presence.

Another time she crept up next to him, bent down, and removed her boob from her blouse so that it was within his line of sight. He lost all concentration as he got a bead on her bosom, at which point she jumped back in feigned shock and innocence...*Naughty Monsieur!*

She had prick teaser down pat.

\*

We enjoyed exploring the narrow streets and corridors of Old San Juan. There was a dark little bar called *El Primitivo*, where you would sit in swings that were suspended by long ropes from the high beams of the ceiling. Lush tropical music played softly in the background. You had to basically feel your way around there because the only light was up at the bar. It made for an intriguing place to take a date.

One night Ally decided on a whim she wanted to go out and walk till we found some music or a jukebox. She put on this trench coat that was a dead ringer for the one Humphrey Bogart wore in *Casablanca*. With nothing else on underneath.

We ascended a little ways to Calle Luna—which had attained the nickname of Street Of The Whores, and turned left. The irony was not lost on me, with Ally nude beneath her thin windbreaker. We ducked into a little place that had a jukebox. A few men were scattered disparately around the bar. We took a table and ordered drinks. *Cuba Libre* for me, as I was into rum and Coke at the time. I checked out the jukebox and saw a Celia Cruz tune on there. I deposited a nickel and when the song began to play we moved together slowly on the little dance floor, with me trying to gauge if any parts of her nakedness were peeping through the half-buttoned coat and enticing the men at the bar. They were definitely taking notice. (Enticing men in bars would turn out to be more than we bargained for on a future occasion—but that comes later.)

Arriving back at the hotel, Ally was antsy. "Hurry up, Ducky," she said as I fumbled with our door key. "I want to hop into bed!"

And with that she wriggled out of the trenchcoat and let it fall to her feet. She was now completely starkers in the hotel corridor. It was still early, and anyone could have happened by. Had they done so, she would have smiled sweetly and issued them a cheery greeting, as if nothing was unusual about her standing in the hallway naked.

*

We were sitting up in bed, sharing a joint. Somewhere during the conversation, the I-Love-You words slipped out of my mouth.

"You don't really know me," Ally said.

"Oh, you mean there's more?"

"I was a junkie."

That turned my head. "I'll shut up and listen," I said.

The doobie dwindled down. Then out.

"There was this guy I stayed with. He kept me...he kept me addicted. Kept me supplied. I was a zombie. I was his slave. He'd have his friends and business acquaintances—I didn't know who they were—over at night. I'd be in my room, sleeping. I'd wake up and there'd be some formless...*mass*...on top of me in the dark. I never saw their faces. He'd tell them to just go on in. Fuck her. She doesn't care. I couldn't leave...he was my only lifeline..."

The way she looked at me, I could see Ally wanted me to despise her for telling me this.

There was a pregnant pause.

"Why are you with me? she said. "I'm such a whore."

I flashed my genuine smile and said, "I *like* whores."

# Chapter 21

## *GIRLS ON THE HALF-SHELL*

There were numerous tourists at the Darlington who visited the Black Angus Steak House just across the road from the hotel, hoping to get a convenient meal. But that wasn't the kind of "steak" they were serving in this dimly lit establishment. I'll admit to having sampled the menu there a time or three—mainly out of boredom—which consisted primarily of South American girls on the halfshell. You'd walk in and immediately be accosted by some pretty young thing, who would get you to buy her a drink, and then sit with you and rub your leg (or something else) while quoting you a price. It was always the same: "Fifteen and six. Fifteen for me, and six for the room."

In the room the lighting would be better, and she usually turned out to be not quite as young nor as pretty as she had originally appeared. No matter. You were there on a lark. Killing time. Trying to fill some empty void for a few moments. She'd wash your tool in the sink, and then you'd get down to business. Sometimes she'd emit a few perfunctory moans, just to try and give you your money's worth.

Once every six months or so, the *policia* would show up there in the morning and they'd haul all the beds out of the place to make it look like they were busting the joint. I'd watch the new beds (or they may have been the same old beds) being delivered the next day, and they'd be up and running again.

That a cheap cathouse could operate so openly just across the street from a big tourist hotel was part of the unique charm and character of San Juan in the late sixties!

# Chapter 22

## *SATURDAY NIGHT'S ALRIGHT FOR FIGHTIN'*

Ally and I wanted to get away for a few days. Just the two of us. I scheduled some vacation days, and we settled on a three day sojourn to Curacao—an intriguing island destination, we thought, 37 miles off the coast of Venezuela.

Before we boarded the plane Ally dropped this disconcerting little tidbit of info on me, in her casual way: she had once been a courier for some underworld concerns. Transporting heroin and cocaine. Should I have been surprised? It all fit into a pattern with the revelations about her previous drug habit.

The aura of intrigue clung to her like cobweb.

I should have seen it coming, I guess. When we tried to clear customs in Curacao, we were invited into a back room for an intimate inspection of or belongings. Could Ally have been on some kind of watch list? And then I thought of something...

OH SHIT!

While I was packing I'd noticed a few tiny marijuana seeds inside my suitcase. Rather than take everything out and repack to get rid of those few tiny seeds, I shrugged it off. I was careless that way. I was careless in a lot of ways that you will learn about later. Anyway, we weren't going to have any trouble.

The customs officials sequestered Ally and me in separate rooms for questioning while they rifled through our bags. Now, in my mind, those tiny seeds were growing into what could sprout into a huge nightmare. Visions of languishing in the slammer on foreign soil indefinitely danced, but not like sugarplums, in my head. This was the meaning of sweating bullets.

They were standard questions. What is the purpose of your visit? How long will you be staying? Are you now, or have you ever been, a depraved hippie freak??? (I made that one up).

After what seemed like an eternity, but must have been about half an hour, our luggage was returned and Ally and I were reunited.

"You are free to go, my friends. Enjoy your stay."

We breathed a sigh of relief. They were looking for bigger barracuda to fry.

*

It was late in the day when we got settled into our accommodations—a bed and breakfast type place with the feel of a private home. I woke the next morning to the sound of goats bleating somewhere in the dense green foliage outside our window. That wasn't what actually woke me. I was having one hell of a sexy dream, I knew that much. And as my eyes fluttered slowly open I wasn't sure if I was awake or still dreaming. Ally was busying herself between my legs. She'd been letting her hair grow and it covered her face (this was a covert operation) as her head bobbed slowly up and down, establishing a rhythm that was turning into the sweetest music I'd ever heard. I'd never woken to something this exquisite before. Ally had more imagination in her thumbnail than most women did in their entire pinky finger. Or something like that.

The day was off on the good foot. I felt it was an omen. There was exploring to do and grub to be rustled up. The island was part of The Netherlands Antilles, and as such the architecture of Willemstad, Curacao was heavily laden with Dutch Colonial influence. We strolled around the historic district and I remarked to Ally that I half expected to see folks clip-clopping around in wooden shoes.

By now it was late in the afternoon and dusk was settling in. We needed to take a load off. We ducked into an airy waterfront bar and grabbed a table. We ordered drinks and were starting to get a buzz on when this swarthy looking older man approached. He was trying to speak to Ally. She wasn't provocatively dressed this night, but she exuded sexuality no matter what she wore. Some women are like that.

"Excuse me, madam...miss...I just want to...*talk* to you..."

The man was gesturing with his hands in a way that made me think he was Italian. He staggered to keep his balance. Drunk on his ass. He seemed not to notice that I was there. I wasn't feeling threatened by him. I'd had to put a guy bigger than me flat on his back on the pavement one night back in Iowa. I sat astride him, pummeling him repeatedly in the face with my fists until 3 guys came along and pulled me off of him. That wasn't my style at all. Not even close. But when the self-preservation instinct kicks in, you do what you have to do.

"You are *byoo-tee-full*...you are *byoo-tee-full*." The inebriated man slurred out the words.

Ally was looking amused. We were both grinning at his buffoonery. It didn't have to turn out the way it did.

A second man approached and grabbed the drunk by the arm. "What is the matter with you? You have *offended* this woman! Stupid Brute!"

And with that he gave the man a shove and he fell backwards onto the floor. The drunk struggled to get to his feet. There was more pushing and shoving. Some of the other men there seemed to want to defend the poor inebriated soul. Pushing and shoving escalated into fisticuffs. It's a classic scene in the old western movies where two cowpokes have an altercation in a saloon and the whole joint explodes.

This was that.

A crowd started gathering outside and some of the curiosity seekers spilled into the place and joined in the fracas. The sea of flailing and cursing humanity surged as one—this way and that—as if it were a giant school of fish.

I grabbed hold of Ally and some angels cleared a pathway for us—there was no other explanation for it—and we beat it out of there to the sound of sirens approaching.

So much fun we were having in Curacao!

The next riot I'd find myself caught up in wasn't going to be nearly as laughable.

# Chapter 23

## IT'S ONLY A GAME, RIGHT?

You can write a memoir without telling your readers exactly where you're coming from and let them try to figure it out on their own. One event follows another. I laughed. I cried. But why? I intend to tell you where I'm coming from so you get a feel for the ashes—or maybe the bottom of the outhouse hole—I rose up from like a very smelly phoenix. Because I want you to see that early beginnings don't have to define you, except maybe in ways that are toughening you up or tearing you down.

I grew up in tiny towns in the midwest where everyone knew your name and your business. If you got on the wrong side of people, it was hard to turn that around. At the age of fourteen, I had developed something of a smart mouth (little did I know then that "smart mouth" would become the key to my livelihood). But on this day, I should have kept it tightly zipped. I was descending the wooden staircase from the pool hall that was the local hangout for teenagers and besotted reprobates as well. A couple of "hoods" (nowadays we'd just call them thugs), grown men in their twenties, were behind me and told me to move out of the way, asshole. I knee-jerk shot something back at them. They grabbed me and beat the shit out of me. If you've ever watched professional wrestling you're familiar with a move called the airplane spin, where one competitor hoists another atop his shoulders, spins around, and lets the guy fly to land where he may. That's what they did to me. Except I didn't have a mat to land on. I hit the hard ground. It felt like my ass was broken. But I didn't cry. I limped away, having just been given a textbook lesson on the kind of people you should never mouth off to in this world. I was a fourteen year-old kid. They were grown men. Degenerates. Still, I guess you're never too young to learn.

The good news was that my ass wasn't busted. But I had some torn ligaments between my collar bone and my shoulder (I just read that it takes a lot of force to tear those ligaments!). I told my old man about it, but I gave him some cock n' bull story about running into the refrigerator in the middle of the night. He didn't buy it. But I felt shame and embarrassment over the incident, and I wasn't going to tell anybody what really happened.

He took me to the local physician, who had just the thing for it. Ol' doc attached some kind of contraption that put on and off pressure onto the area, squeezing it and squeezing it, and making it hurt a ton more. It didn't help. I think that quack was a sadist.

It was autumn. I was a freshman in high school, so I went out for the football team. Not that I would have been a great football player, though I might have been okay—I was fairly athletic. But in a little town all the high school boys went out for football. They needed the bodies, and it was the thing to do. I never told my coach that I had the injury, which still hadn't significantly healed. I thought I could tough it out. One of the drills in practice was that you had to run full speed against a blocking dummy and slam your shoulder into it. The pain of that when it hit my bad side was excruciating. But I never said a word about it. I tried to hang in there as long as I could. I knew it was making my injury worse. Under the circumstances, there was nothing I could do but quit the team, or explain what had happened to me. And I wasn't going to do the latter. Stubborn little bastard.

Word gets around in these wee small towns like poop through a goose. My peers crucified me. QUITTER! LETTING THE TEAM DOWN! From then on, I was a pariah. I had zero friends. The kids took up a mantra: *You're worthless...you'll never amount to a pile of dog shit!* Could things get any worse? Yes they could. I had developed a severely nasty acne condition. One day I was this nice looking kid, and the next I was Pizza Face. They made up choice nicknames for me. They'd sit behind me on the school bus and snicker. Most of them were going to live and die within a small radius of where they were at that moment.

Bullying wasn't a word we thought of much in those days. I felt I was just taking what I had coming to me. I knew why it was happening and it had been my choice to let it go in that direction. It went on more or less like that for a couple of years, until I moved away from there.

I'd found a secret place deep in the core of my being where no one could touch me. I developed a titanium shell and after a while all that shit just bounced right off me. It was the only way I could survive.

# Chapter 24

## CLAP FOR THE WOLF MAN

I worked a day shift on Saturdays at the station to break things up and allow me to have two nights off a week. And as you know, I never knew who was going to walk through that portal at Penthouse One.

I was doing my Saturday thing and this guy came in and announced his name as Robert Smith. Would it be alright if he used our production room for a bit to record some tapes to send back to his own station? I said no problem. I showed him the basics and he went in there and got down to it.

Our production room wasn't completely soundproof, and what I heard coming out of there was a very loud, and a very credible impersonation of Wolfman Jack. I knew that Robert Smith was the Wolfman's real name, so I rolled my eyes and thought this guy is playing it to the hilt. He was clean shaven and his hair was slicked back. He didn't look like the Wolfman. Well...he did have the same shape face. The same build. Had he been wearing his trademark goatee he might have looked quite a bit like the guy who initially got me to dreaming about what it might be like to be a wacky personality on the radio. I'd lay in my bed late at night in that lonely Iowa farmhouse, pulling in the Wolfman's booming signal from Mexico on my transistor radio.

After about an hour of his boisterous antics—the gravelly

voice, the laugh, the whole thing—"Robert Smith" thanked me politely for the use of the studio. And then he was gone. There was no doubt in my mind that he was one of those eccentric folks who walks into a radio station with no one else around and starts doing Wolfman Jack.

Except who the fuck does that?

I've had a lot of years to ruminate on it, and my gut tells me now that he was the real deal. My regret is that I let him get away without saying something meaningful like: *YOU made me laugh so hard I almost ran off a bridge, man!*

# Chapter 25

## *SIMON SAYS*

I would dare Ally to do things and see if she would follow through, as a perverse way of proving her love for me. I knew there was a point at which I would become insanely jealous. I wanted to goad her right up to that line but not cross it.

It was a Sunday morning and we were being Sunday lazy. Ally was still in her nightgown. I told her to go over to the window that faced Boulevard Del Valle below, open it, and expose her tits until someone in the street below came along and saw her. She did so without hesitation. A man walked past and she called to him in her gregarious way, like an airline hostess waving from the door of the plane just before departure. "HI...HELLO THERE," she giggled.

I watched from behind the curtain of an adjacent window pane. The man looked up for a moment, saw this topless woman leaning out of a hotel room window, and had to figure she was a working girl trying to drum up business. And on a Sunday morning when church bells were ringing...*Ave Maria!*

Another time we were at the beach and I said to her, "See that guy over there? I want you to call him a penis in Spanish."

She let it fly: *Mira...pinga!* The guy pretended not to hear. Obviously a working girl trying to drum up business.

One night we took out my Harley, Ally clinging to me with

her arms around my waist. She was wearing a dress—not a good choice on a bike (I don't remember if she had any panties on). A carload of "good feelers" pulled up beside us. They rolled down their windows and started hooting at her. The dress billowed up in the wind, exposing her legs and upper thighs. I didn't catch all the words in Spanish these guys were directing her way, but it didn't take a great imagination to pick up the gist. It seemed to be a cultural kind of thing. I looked back at her to see how she was taking it, and she seemed genuinely chagrined. Well that was different. (I wasn't rattled by it...me and my boys had done a lot of that sort of thing in my latter years of high school. Thus the quaint midwestern expression, "good feelers!")

Now, I don't mean to give the impression that between the two of us, Ally got all the attention. As I walked down the street one sunny day, wearing a pair of shorts—and shorts were shorter in those days—here came another carload of local dudes. One of them called out to me, "You have beautiful legs!"

There were lots of pervy guys vocalizing out of car windows in those days. But I *did* have beautiful legs, and I felt flattered by the comment—his gender notwithstanding.

Entering the hotel pool one day, this gal—I'd seen her there before with a Gomer Pyle hat pulled around her ears—said loud enough for me to hear: *It's...THE BODY!* I wasn't super muscular or anything like that, but I was toned and tan. Kinda like Frankie Avalon in *Beach Blanket Bingo*. Oh, and did I tell you that I had it *all*? That I had Ally and I had my beautiful legs and I was crazy Charlie Brown on the radio and I had the world by the balls? But of course, I didn't know it. Like anyone caught up in the grand delusions of youth, I couldn't envision a time when things would be any different.

# Chapter 26

## *BEAT ME DADDY, EIGHT TO THE BAR*

Our first fight. I can't remember what it was about, but I'll guarantee you it was something stupid. We had each gone to bed pissed off. It was eating at me and I couldn't sleep. I got up and paced around. I wanted to do something nasty. Something to needle her and *really* piss her off.

She was having no similar trouble snoozing. She was zonked out. I crept up next to her side of the bed. She was lying on her side, facing inward. I dropped my shorts and...well...I...uh...masturbated on her hair. (Score one more for the bastard in me.) Her tresses were shoulder length and there was plenty of it to cover. And though I'd been stealthy about this sneak attack, she woke up.

"What the *fuck* are you doing?"

"I came in your hair," I said matter of factly.

She looked at me in astonishment. "Jesus Christ...you sonofabitch!"

She stormed off to the bathroom and turned on the shower. "Gonna Wash That Man Right Out Of My Hair," that old classic tune, started playing in my head.

In the morning we didn't talk about it. But it seemed to reset something. We both acknowledged that the trivial thing we were being pissy about wasn't worth being pissy about. And she must have thought: *Gee, if he's gonna beat off in my hair, I must have hurt his feelings.*

I wouldn't recommend this as a reconciliation tactic though guys, as your results may vary.

# Chapter 27

## *BRAIN FART*

In all my tenure at WBMJ, Bob Bennett only reprimanded me one time. I might have been a little too high that night. I came out of a record with this: "There you have The Beatles with 'I'm A Loser'...I listen to WHOA!" It's a cardinal rule in radio that you don't mention your competing stations on the air. But that wasn't the half of it.

I told you that Sally Jessy (Raphael) was doing the morning show at WHOA in what was her initial foray into the broadcasting biz. Shortly after that snarky comment left my lips, Uncle Bob was on the phone. He told me that he was driving Sally home from a dinner engagement they'd had together, and (of course) WBMJ was on the car radio. Sally had heard my egregious remark. She was appalled and embarrassed. My boss made me feel like an ass, which I was. It was a needed reminder for me that there were limits—lines you shouldn't cross—even on the Charlie Brown show.

Sally never spoke to me after that. But then, she'd never spoken to me before that either.

# Chapter 28

## *BIRDS FLY IN THE FALL*

As autumn approached the winds of change were buffeting Ally and me. She would shortly be returning to the mainland for her fall semester of school. That was the deal from the start.

On the night before she left, we visited our little Italian place. We always liked to drink Chianti there. We'd order a bottle and get a buzz on, at which point her foot would often find my nether region beneath the table. On this night the wine, and the occasion, was bittersweet. And no feet.

Ally could see that I was down in the mouth—though I'd tried to conceal it. She touched my arm and said, "There there, Ducky, it will be alright. I'll be back for Christmas break."

That was the plan. We were too much a part of each other now not to keep this thing going. Nothing was mentioned about sexual fidelity in the interim. We were both adults (loosely speaking). We didn't need to make any fifties style adolescent promises, sealed with a kiss. Meantime, I was going to have a few months to kill, and I would need to get creative with that.

# Chapter 29

## *SOCK IT TO ME BABY*

Mitch Ryder ("Devil With A Blue Dress On" and other hot rockin' hits of the sixties) was in town and came up to the station to promote an outdoor concert he was doing on the island. Ryder was still hot at this point—at least the clingy young groupie he brought along with him thought so. He was there to voice a spot that would run on WBMJ to help get the word out about his upcoming performance. Should have been simple enough.

He was in studio B and I was across the glass from him to engineer the session. He stepped up to the mic and I gave him the hand signal to go for it. As he began to speak, his waif-like friend began crawling all over him. (She was wearing a blue dress, as I recall.) She pawed and smothered him with kisses as he tried to speak. He'd start, then stop half way through the reading and start again because she wouldn't leave him alone. It's hard to concentrate when someone is essentially dry humping you while you're trying to work. And he wasn't exactly discouraging her. I thought for a moment we might be witnessing some real X-rated stuff here. What could have taken five minutes stretched to forty-five. Finally, he ordered her to go sit and be good, which she did with a pouty face.

What is it about music, and those who create it—and in my case even those who disseminate it on the radio—that brings out the beast of animal sexuality in otherwise good little girls and boys? The answer is that music is not only a powerful drug, it cuts through all the bullshit layers of language—with its inherent potential for distortion and deception—and works directly upon the emotions and the heart. It is our highest and most honest form of communication. Indeed, music is the only thing that can truly bring us together—regardless of religious, political, or ethnic affiliations. In the end, it is the only thing that will save us. If there is any chance for us to be saved.

\*

The most lyrical songwriter of the era—in my not so humble opinion—was Jimmy Webb. The guy didn't just wear his heart on his sleeve—he wiped his tears and his snotty nose with it. Webb was behind a slew of hits for various artists, including:

The Worst That Could Happen...Brooklyn Bridge

All I Know...Art Garfunkel

Up Up And Away...Fifth Dimension

And these Glen Campbell favorites:

Wichita Lineman

Galveston

Where's The Playground Suzie

By The Time I Get To Phoenix (Johnny Rivers had the better version of it—Campbell had the hit).

But Webb's crowning achievement was "MacArthur Park." That line about leaving the cake out in the rain...that's poetry, man! Richard Harris was the only one with the proper sense of pathos in his voice to do the song justice, and a stunning tour-de-force musical arrangement turned it into a classic.

I remember the first time I heard it—forever etched in my mind. Bob Bennett grabbed me and steered me into the production room and said I want to play something for you. He put the needle to the groove, and we listened with rapt attention. He knew what was coming. Richard Harris emoting his heart out...and then that *kick-ass* instrumental bridge hit me like a pie in the face—a banana creme pie, my favorite! Uncle Bob looked like a little mechanical Christmas elf...his feet moving in rhythm to the beat...head swiveling from side to side with a Cheshire cat grin...me sitting there with mouth agape—and the song wasn't nearly over yet!

We'd shared a moment. And we'd found a song that almost made us brothers.

*

With Ally out of the picture for the time being, I was reconnecting with "The Boys." (I'd soon be reconnecting with the girls as well.) It was my Saturday night off, and a few of us reprobates from the station went out for a night of fun. We boozed it up pretty good, and as the evening wore on we decided to head back to Penthouse One to see what mischief we could get into. Maybe harass whatever part-timer was on the air. On the way over we heard "Satisfaction" by The Rolling Stones, and decided we were going to record our own version of the song!

I rummaged around in our music library and found an instrumental version of the song—pretty lame on its own, but with our voices added we could turn it into something really hot. Hell, we might even play it on the radio if it turned out good! I set a voice level on the guys so we would blend in just right with the music. I rolled tape on the Ampex machine, started the record, and ran around from the production room to studio B to join in with the others. We would take turns on the verses (we knew the song by heart) and then all join in and belt out the chorus. For my part I would give it my guttural funky blues treatment. The others would bring their own inimitable styles. We did a few takes and were eager to hear the finished product...

We made our way back into the prod room—burping, farting, and laughing —your normal sloppy drunk stuff. I started the tape and we sat there grinning stupidly. It wasn't exactly reminiscent of the Stones...no, it was someone else. "We sound kinda like Paul Revere & The Raiders!" I said.

"That's it!" everybody chimed in. "Paul Revere!" Who knew we would be this good? Maybe we'd form a group and call ourselves *The Strapping Jocks* or something clever like that. Anyway, we'd had our fun and our night of male bonding and camaraderie and now it was time to head home.

The following night I went back to listen to the tape again. I was stunned...at how awful it was! Funny...silly...yes...but Paul Revere had ridden away on his horse. It was like going to bed with a beautiful blonde and waking up with Willem Dafoe beside you.

I would have to inform the guys we'd need to put our plans for musical stardom on hold for now.

# Chapter 30

## *FLASHBACK: I'M IN WITH THE OUT CROWD*

At thirteen, I strapped my transistor radio onto the handlebars of my bicycle and I was good to go from summer sun-up to sundown and often into the night. I lived on that bike, and I was intuitive enough to understand that the music, which accompanied me everywhere, was the thing that was going to save me. I wasn't sure just how yet, but at the right time a signpost would point the way.

Later on in high school, after I'd moved away from that tiny town to a bigger little town, I had my own posse of misfits. We called ourselves "The '69ers" (heh heh). I even had some membership cards made up. High school was totally clique-ish. There was a caste system. The kids whose parents belonged to the country club didn't associate with the likes of us. And that was fine. We were proud to be in with the Out Crowd. The only thing you needed to be in the '69ers was a crude sense of humor and a soldier of fortune-like sense of adventure.

There was a radio station I listened to night and day—KSO in Des Moines. There was a guy on there named Dick Vance who made me chuckle every day. He'd have his wife call in—he called her "The Sweater Girl" because she filled out a sweater so well—and he'd ask her what they were having for dinner that night. She always answered: GARBAGE! We'd make pilgrimages to Des

Moines to go to their studios. The deejays were encased in a fishbowl booth that looked out onto the street. Fans could come up and see the deejay at work and make faces at him, or write out a request and hold it up to the glass and he'd play it if it wasn't some piece of shit by Kate Smith.

KSO's competing station—KIOA—had a similar set up. That kind of accessibility—I thought it was cool. These guys were showmen. They were in the *entertainment* biz! And it was laying the groundwork for my own sensibilities of what the medium was supposed to be about.

# Chapter 31

## *BACK TO THE FUTURE*

One night I found myself in a dimly lit club with "Open My Eyes" by The Nazz—Todd Rundgren's first group—and his phase-shifting voice raining down on me from high mounted speakers. I was tripping, and the song was sublime for the moment. I had run into a musician acquaintance of mine there. Larry—whose locks came down to his shoulders—sat across the table from me. He was beaming.

His words floated in the air like a kind of psychedelic alphabet soup. "I'm getting this band together, man," he said. "All these great musicians!"

"Wow, man," I said. You gonna play here on the island?"

"We're gonna play here...we're gonna play New York...*everywhere*, man!"

"That's heavy, man!"

"Yeah!"

Larry was morphing into a Jesus-like figure across from me. Considering where my head was at, that was pretty wild. His confidence, his sense of resolve was contagious. We were grinning from ear to shining ear.

In the following days I would find him getting cozy with an old ex-paramour of mine, Carla, at my apartment. She and I were on friendly terms, and she was residing there for the time being. I say friendly, except that right after she got up in the morning she would call me every filthy, degrading name in the book. *Asshole! Turdsucker!* It was her way of greeting the new day, and perhaps getting a few still unresolved feelings about me off her chest. After she had her coffee, she was all sweetness and light.

Larry and Carla were stretched out on my living room rug, making goo-goo eyes at each other. It was fine with me. If I could facilitate a little more happiness in the world by being a good host, I was up for it. As I walked out the door I said to them, "Be good, kids!"

We all had a good laugh.

*Larry Harlow went on to become a Grammy winning bandleader, record producer and piano player for the legendary Fania All-Stars, with more than a hundred albums to his credit—fifty of them his own.*

# Chapter 32

## *THE UGLY TRUTH*

Rueben Figueroa was a child actor who played one of Alan Arkin's sons in the film *Popi* (1969), which also starred Rita Moreno. In '68 the film crew was on the island doing some shooting for the movie, which was set it Puerto Rico and New York. I ran into the crew at the Darlington, where they were doing some filming around the pool area (I remember the cameraman zooming in for a super close-up shot of this chick's bikini clad ass, but I don't think that shot made it into the movie). I met Reuben there, a precocious kid who was on his way to making a name for himself in the movies. He seemed curious about radio and what I did, so I'd sit and chat with him sometimes. One day we were having lunch together at the hotel coffee shop, A couple stools down from us was this loud, fat guy...*The Ugly American.*

"Speak English!" he barked at the servers behind the counter. They'd spoken to him in English when they took his order, but he was getting pissed off because they were conversing in Spanish among themselves! I was appalled, and so was young Reuben.

"You know, this is *their* country, not ours," I said to him as politely as I could. He just grumbled under his breath...*grumble, grumble, grumble.*

The phenomenon of The Ugly American can perhaps be best explained with an analogy about the game of soccer, or "futbol" as it is known throughout much of the world. The game is hugely popular nearly everywhere but in the U.S., which has a mild interest in it at best (except when our teams are winning the World Cup—then all the fair weather fans come out of the woodwork). It's a fun sport to play, but it's mind numbingly boring to watch. The teams go up and down the field...up and down...and nothing much happens. That's why a typical final score is 1-0, and often matches end up in a zero to zero tie. All of that work and look what you have to show for it. The reason for this is the debilitating rule that you can only use your feet or your head, but not your hands. It's like what American football would be if you could only use your hands and not your feet. Makes the kick-off extremely difficult that way.

    A while back I pondered what makes the game so popular worldwide and not so much in the states. And then it hit me. Americans are into instant gratification. We want it bigger, faster, and we want it now! So we like sports where there's a lot of action and a lot of scoring, such as basketball and football. BAM! Another made basket or touchdown. Yell your damn fool head off and guzzle your beer. We want cheap, crappy fast food. As long as we don't have to wait. We think we're the center of the universe—that's why our triumphant sports teams are crowned *world champions* when no teams from other countries even participated! There's a sense of arrogance that often drips like sweat off a fat guy at a coffee shop in San Juan demanding that everyone speak

English because he's never made an effort to understand anything else.

By contrast, people in poorer countries are not used to getting what they want so easily. In many cases they're not used to getting what they want at all. They toil day after day with no real reward other than subsistence. They're used to waiting in lines. Bread lines and such. All of this has developed something in them called *patience* and *tolerance*. And there you have the key to soccer. It doesn't seem boring to them to watch two teams go up and down the field and nothing is happening. It just feels like regular life. And when something DOES finally happen...a team scores a goal...it's like the heavens open up and the broadcast announcer is shouting GOOOAAAAALLL like a freakin' maniac and the crowd is going wild! A level of passion unleashed that many westerners may not understand. But I think I understand it. I hear it in the music. I see it in the faces. The so-called "poorer" places of the world are often the richest in art, culture and tradition. And I have always felt more at home there than in the "white-bread" world from whence I sprang.

# Chapter 33

## *GOT GAME*

I'd moved from the San Cristobal Hotel—it was too lonely there with Ally gone—and taken up residence at the Darlington, which was in the process of being renovated and renamed the Borinquen. I guess that fit better, because that was the name the natives had given to the island back in the days of Columbus.

I could hang out at the pool for most of the afternoon, and when 7 o'clock rolled around my commute to work was a thirty second elevator ride up to the studio, which I often made without changing out of my swim trunks and sandals—ready to boogie the night away come what may.

Today I checked in a little early because I wanted to catch the receptionist, Diane, before she left. Diane had been spending quite a few of her lunch breaks down at my apartment. Just a quick ride down in the elevator, a quickie at my place, and a quick ride back to work. We weren't romantically involved. We were just following our God-given instincts. Our common denominator was proximity, which is much more of a matchmaker than the moon and the stars ever were. Let's say there's someone in a far corner of the world who would be a perfect match for you or me. It doesn't matter because we're never going to meet that person. We hook up with those who live in our own space—at work, at school, or by the pool. And Diane was there everyday looking fetching behind that reception desk.

"You missed him," she said.

"Who?"

"Bob Hope."

"The Big Guy is in town?"

"Yeah...came through here with his huge entourage."

"That figures. The more famous you are, the bigger your entourage."

"He recorded some promos for you and the guys."

"Wow...Bob Hope promoting me on the air. I've officially arrived!"

"He was real nice." Her voice shifted into intimate mode. "He wanted me to come back to his hotel with him."

"Really!"

"I didn't go. And I'm not going."

"You may want to reconsider...you might get a big raise out of it."

"You *A-Hole!*" she said in her exaggerated east coast accent. (Think Fran Drescher saying: You A-hole!)

Later, when I thought about it, I was struck by the irony. Mr. Hope had a reputation as a womanizer, and I've no doubt he got his share (even though he was married). But on this occasion I had beaten him out for the affections of a lovely lady. You see, it's not always about who's got the wealth and fame.

Sometimes it's just about who got game.

# Chapter 34

## *WHO AM I? (OOH OOH, OOH OOH)*

I popped into a cafeteria style place in the old city one day, thinking I would have a quiet leisurely lunch. I carried my food tray to a small two person table and took a load off. A young short-haired woman was moving through the line. I observed her with an appreciation for her figure and her pleasant face. Then she was walking with her tray, moving in my direction. There was no shortage of available tables, but she came right up to mine and said, "Do you mind if I sit with you?"

Ever gracious, I said, "Not at all."

She settled in and I generated a bit of small talk. Perhaps good fortune was smiling at me over a plate of rice and beans. And then the inevitable question came up, "What do you do?"

I hesitated for a moment. Then I came out with it. "I'm on the radio," I said. "On WBMJ." I saw the raised eyebrows. The skeptical look. "You listen to it?"

"Uh-huh."

"I'm Charlie Brown."

"Charlie Brown?" she spat: "You? HAH!" Her tone had rapidly switched from skeptical to downright hostile.

"No, really."

"YOU are not Charlie Brown. Charlie is a BIG BIG man!"

It was true that I had a baritone voice. It was your classic "radio" voice. I suppose a lot of folks might have conjured up an image of Hulk Hogan's double. I was medium height and medium build. I was a normal looking person (okay, a normal looking *hippie*), and that clashed with her preconceived ideas about reality.

She shook her head in disgust. "What is wrong with you? Why are you telling me this?"

"I-I can take you to the station. You want to go to the radio station?"

And with that the young woman got up, left the remaining food on her plate, and stomped out of there. Imagine the *balls* of this guy trying to pick her up with some cock and bull story like that!

In a way she was right. I was not Charlie Brown at that *moment*. Charlie was my alter-ego. Off the air, I was the mild mannered sort (kinda like Superman and Clark Kent!).

The flip side of that was I would sometimes get calls while I was on the air from girls I didn't know. *Hey, remember me? We went out together Saturday night?* Uh...no we didn't. There were guys out there who were impersonating me! I shuddered to think about what they might be doing to these women, or the jerks they were being in my name.

Mistaken identity is one thing. *Identity theft* with the ripping off of serious funds and attempted murder is a whole other kettle of sushi. That little misadventure is still to come. Stay tuned kids!

# Chapter 35

## *FLASHBACK: SCHOOL DAZE*

High school graduation was coming up, and I was still an aimless soul in my mind.

What was I going to do? Go to college? I had no love for the idea. I had been in some plays—small parts with only a few spoken lines, but enough for me to begin developing a taste for being in the spotlight.

In study hall I'd spend my time penning satirical, off-color poetry (a drunken Santa Claus busting up furniture on Christmas Eve because no cookies had been left out for him) when I should have been concentrating on school work. In class I'd pass these literary gems around—the poems would circulate from classmate to sniggering classmate—up and down the aisles while "Teach" was up there doing his blah blah. One day my English instructor intercepted one of my missives, snatching it out of a student's hands. He looked at it...began to laugh...turned red-faced because he knew he wasn't supposed to do that...and went on a half hour tirade about how such trash was the product of a sick mind! It was then and there that I began to consider the idea that maybe I could become some kind of entertainer.

# Chapter 36

## *UP ON THE ROOF*

The roof garden at Penthouse One was a romantic spot to present female visitors with a panoramic view of San Juan at night. There would be numerous opportunities for getting cozy, and more. It also presented me with a little mischievous fun. As I mentioned, I could view the entire pool and pool bar area from there. I'd scope for hotel guests sitting and chatting directly below. I wanted those who were fully and finely dressed, perhaps getting ready for a night on the town.

There was a garden hose hooked up out there to water the plants. I'd take the hose and drape it over the ledge, turn it on, and direct a stream of water down upon those unsuspecting heads. The sitting ducks would jump up, confused because it was a cloudless night, jerking their heads around to try and identify the source of their impromptu shower. By then I had ducked out of sight and they were never the wiser.

Into each life a little rain must fall...all part of your unique island experience here at the Borinquen Hotel! No extra charge.

\*

Women were falling from the sky as well, and I was Gene Kelly doing that song and dance number from *Singin' In The Rain*. In another classic film, Clint Eastwood played a radio deejay who gets a call from a mysterious woman who breathes the words "play misty for me" into the phone. She turns out to be a psycho who tries to kill him. So imagine the hair on the back of my neck doing a dance when I received a copycat call at work one night from an equally mysterious woman uttering those same words. In the film the psycho woman's name was Evelyn. And you guessed it, this dame's name was Evelyn too. I scoffed at that, but she was telling the truth. It was a cute way to start off a romance, because she wasn't a nightmare—she was a deejay's wet dream!

If you want eerie, though, there was Elaine, a half Asian cutie who was sitting behind the reception desk at the ad agency I did some freelance work for (she could have been mistaken for Leslie Caron). When our eyes met, she looked like she'd seen a ghost. In fact she had. She told me I was a dead ringer for her deceased husband. Morbid curiosity got the best of us, and for a while I tried to fill his bedroom slippers. Did she want me for me, or for the stand-in fantasy role I could play? In the end it got too creepy for her, and she ran.

But for a while there Evelyn was dropping by the station on Tuesday and Thursday nights, while Elaine visited on Wednesdays and Fridays. I had to stagger them that way and be sure not to get the dates mixed up so they both didn't show up on the same night. We played out on the roof garden beneath the stars while a long song was on the turntable. The sixteen minute version of "In-A-Gadda-Da-Vida" by Iron Butterfly was a handy one for such occasions.

And then there was Lana. She showed up at the radio station one day with two large suitcases, looking like a lost waif. My old childhood friend, Danel, knew her and had sent her down from the states because he thought—for some odd reason—that I could arrange an abortion for her. The term *Roe v Wade* was not yet in our common vernacular, and wouldn't be until 1973 when the practice would be decriminalized nationwide in the states. There were, of course, back alley providers. I guess Daniel thought she'd be more likely to find one here in the Caribbean, where "anything goes." But I didn't know anyone who even knew anyone who might know someone who would provide that kind of service, and I told her that straightaway. Ah well, she wasn't showing yet, so we decided to make the best of her time there regardless.

We had come from the beach and were meandering along the Condado when a motorcycle cop pulled up beside us and informed us that Lana couldn't be on the street looking like *that*. She was in her bikini—tame by today's standards—and I had seen plenty of tourists navigating these same paths in similar attire. Then I realized he wasn't referring to the bikini, but the way she was *filling out* the bikini. June had come and gone, but Lana—who resembled Jayne Mansfield up top—was busting out all over. Motorists could smash into one another from craning their necks and gawking, the cop said with a straight face. Chaos could ensue! I removed the shirt I was wearing over my swim trunks and gave it to her to put on. The civic-minded embodiment of the law allowed that would be acceptable, and we pushed on back to my place.

We made it that night, haphazardly and half-assedly, with her declaring in the middle of it, "Ya gotta understand this doesn't mean much to me because I still love David!" (right...just not enough to bear his spawn).

In the early morn Nancy showed up out of the blue (do we really have to go into Nancy? I mean, I did, but that's beside the point). She cooed at me through the slats of my bedroom window. And then..."YOU BASTARD!" She spat the words nearly into my ear, and stomped off when Lana raised her sleepy head, waking the pious Puerto Rican lady next door who had already given me dirty looks for the debauchery she *suspected* was ongoing at my abode.

I never saw Nancy again, but what's a young buck trying to live in the moment to do?

Sometime after that, Daniel informed me that Lana had done a photo spread for one of the cheesier men's magazines. Not once, but twice. I figured she must have found her back alley provider, as being in the family way is rather hard to conceal in your birthday suit. Just a small bump, you might say, on her road to sleazy stardom. I thought about trying to locate some back issues to see if I could find her...but then I said why bother. Been there. Done that.

*

I would see this guy sometimes—shuffling through the hotel,

making his way to the pool bar, where he would try to strike up conversations with some of the young chicks. He had to be near sixty—which seemed as ancient as the pyramids to me at the time. Hair slicked back and kind of greasy, with a thin Cesar Romero mustache. Usually wore a leisure suit (remember those?). Whatever woman he would plop next to on the stool would listen politely to him for a few minutes, and then politely excuse herself before things got really creepy.

It made me sad. Because I could see myself in him. Like a visit from The Ghost of Christmas Future. I said: *God...don't let me be that guy!* Don't let me be some doddering old fuck, still hitting on the sweet young things with zero chance of scoring.

That's why (remembering Siddhartha) I felt it was imperative to get as much of this skirt chasing out of my system as possible...while I was still in good enough shape to catch up to the faster ones.

# Chapter 37

## *RETURN TO ME*

Autumn gave way to winter. Not that we noticed it much on the island. Those changes were subtle. Average temperatures in the summer were in the nineties. Average temperatures in the winter were in the eighties. A little more muggy in the summer. A little less muggy in the winter. It was more about the psychological changes that people went through during the holidays. But I was on a high. Ally would soon be returning.

I'd moved into a roomy shotgun apartment on Del Casse street just off of Ashford Avenue in the Condado. It was a short walk up to Las Nereidas Restaurant, an all night bistro where you could park your butt with a beer and a sandwich and see who you might run into. That may have been where I hooked up with Candy, a little dark-eyed, dark-haired, dark-skinned (she was dark) young thing who was into Scientology.

She took me over to the Scientology headquarters. She told me that the object of it was to get "clear." I let her give me a test where I was supposed to hold onto a couple beer cans hooked up by strings to a box with some kind of meter on it (at first I thought we were going to talk through them like the beer can and string telephones we used to play with as kids). She asked me a few questions and the meter was supposed to pick up some kind of vibrations, sort of a poor man's lie detector.

WOW—I had a lot of potential—but there were a few issues Scientology could help me with until I eventually got clear. I wasn't sure how I was supposed to feel when I reached that state, but it would all become clear. In time. Hey, I had an open mind. Not many folks had heard about Scientology at that point, and we were still a long ways from drinking the Kool-Aid at Jonestown, and Tom Cruise busting the springs on Oprah's couch, all of which opened our eyes to the inherent dangers of cults that coerced their followers to cut off contact with anyone considered to be a non-believer.

I hung around with Candy some after that, and one night we ended up back at my place. It happened to be the night before Ally's return. I had gone all out in decorating the place festively for the holidays. I really hoped she would like it.

I didn't expect Candy to ask me if she could stay over. It had gotten late and there would be no buses back to her abode. I told her she could stay, but I was wary about it. She didn't ask if she could hop into bed with me. But there we were, and she had removed all her clothes. It had to go one way or the other. I told her flat out that my girlfriend was arriving from the states tomorrow, and that I was excited about seeing her again. And that it wasn't meant as a slight to her, Candy, but I couldn't. Couldn't do the deed with her. Yes, I had been a naughty boy in Ally's absence, but on the night before our reunion, I was going to keep myself pure for her.

Candy took it well because she was a seeker. She was working on herself. Getting her head together, man. Gazing into her belly button and contemplating the meaning of the universe. A lot of folks from our generation were in that same lane as we traveled along that uncertain, dog turd strewn path of life. (Anyway, rack up another point for the "nice" version of me. Are you keeping score? I've lost track.)

\*

Ally and I picked up right where we had left off. We were made for each other. The easy laughter. We saw the irony and the twisted humor in everything. I had her record a gag radio spot that we wrote together—she portrayed a gal who was advertising her services to other women who were having their periods. Just call and she'd be happy to hop right onto their man's cock to tide him over until the monthly curse subsided. It wasn't anything I could play on the air, but we had fun with it. She had a real creative side to her.

My place was festively bedecked, so we decided to throw a Christmas party. Most of those we invited were colleagues and the management staff from the radio station, and they were free to bring a guest or two along. I picked up a few bottles of cheap scotch (I really should have splurged more on that), we had finger foods, and WBMJ was booming on the radio.

When the guests began to arrive, they didn't know what to make of it. Ally was wearing a French maid's costume with her cleavage spilling out the top of it (stopping just short of nipplage—after all, these were my business associates!). I, on the other hand, may have carried it too far. I had on a pair of semi-transparent red silk briefs...and nothing else (they *were* a festive color!). So as people filtered in—a lot of the men in jackets and ties, and the women nattily dressed as well—they were greeted by two freaky but intriguing hosts, and the vibe was anything goes. It gave us the opportunity to explore our exhibitionistic sides (which Ally had already been doing in spades). I realize now that what we were doing was essentially performance art, like when normal looking people gather in a museum to watch some slightly unbalanced "artiste" do some disquietingly bizarre things.

Most of the folks there seemed to pick up on the joke. Some of them were even tasting my crummy scotch. Ally and I were being the perfect convivial hosts. John Scott the newsman was there, my boss Bob Bennett was there, and the new receptionist at the station—a Puerto Rican girl named Olivia—was there. At one point she called me over and said, "*Why* are you dressed like that, Charlie Brown?" But I noticed her eyes never left my semi-transparent crotch. And there was a straightlaced looking guy in a coat and tie chatting up Bob Bennett at the booze table. He was obviously a business contact of some sort. He looked askance at me and I heard him say, "How can they let someone like that in here?"

Uncle Bob just shrugged his shoulders and said, "It's *his*

party!"

The guy walked out in a huff.

# Chapter 38

## *BOB, TED, CAROL, AND ALICE REVISITED*

Frequent personnel turnover is common in radio (it's an itinerant business) and WBMJ was no exception. Ric Roberts and Johnny Ringo had both returned to the mainland. Some of the names of those who came afterward were: Marty Malo, Phil Baker, Scott Brady (my good buddy), Moonshadow, Davey O'Donnell, and a guy I'll identify only by the initials "A.J." (you'll understand why).

A.J. was a southern boy who had taken over the midday shift. He wore a goatee that he liked to refer to as "my womb broom." Ally and I wanted to broaden our social circle, so we invited A.J. to come up with a date and the four of us would go out for dinner and drinks. He picked up a blonde from somewhere (the blonde repository?) named Kathy. Kathy was on the tall and thin side and looked like she had enough floozy in her to fit right into our little foursome.

After our wine and dine, we ended up back at my place for a nightcap. We were all pretty buzzed, and when A.J. and Kathy started climbing all over each other on the sofa, Ally and I discreetly retired to the bedroom to become similarly engaged. As we were wriggling out of our duds, Ally said, "You think we should invite them in here with us?" It seemed like the neighborly thing to do, so I said okay, let's call them in. I wasn't sure what we were getting ourselves into, or what I wanted to get into (other than Ally), but there we were. A.J. and his blonde occupying the left side of the bed and me and Ally on the right—each staying in our lanes for the moment.

I glanced over at our guests and they were engaged in what might be politely described as intercourse. I gave Ally a gentle hint (by clambering astride her) that we ought to follow suit. We started in, but she seemed distracted. At one point Ally had shifted onto her side...A.J. was similarly positioned facing away from her...and her naked ass began rubbing up against his naked ass! This made me jealous, so I turned Ally onto her back and proceeded to give it to her with a vengeance. She had me all confused about where we were at. It would have been easy for me to tap A.J. on the shoulder and say SWITCHEROO! I could have had sloppy seconds with his partner, and he...*he would have been fucking Ally with me watching!* Maybe that's what she was figuring on. I wasn't ready for it. I was caught in that sexual no man's land between being highly titillated by the situation, and feeling the helpless jealousy of the cuckold.

The evening was spent. We were spent. Ally and I escorted our guests to the door, where my girlfriend stood full frontal before my colleague—the light shining in on her from Del Casse street—giving him a great view of the scenery, if he hadn't peeked at it before. Her "hills like white elephants" and her moss bedecked valley. Ally displayed herself so proudly. And so nonchalantly.

She was made for the spotlight.

*

I would often relax by the Borinquen Hotel pool before work while Ally was out shopping or otherwise cultivating her independent side to balance the scales a bit. There would always be some pleasant scenery to behold beside the pool. I knew that I loved Ally. It wasn't about that. It was about being twenty-three years old and living in a tourist mecca where temptation lurked at every turn. It was about undulating waves of sunlight dancing upon the water. The breeze flirting with the fronds of the surrounding palms. The tourist chick giving you the eye from across the way.

And so I met this little short-haired blonde from Baltimore—she had a kind of Twiggy look to her—while she was down for the week with a couple of her friends. One thing led to another and lo and behold I was on the bed with her up in her room. We had our clothes on. Making out. It was innocent stuff. I'll admit I slipped my hand inside her shorts and she let it linger there while my nimble fingers did some exploring. I guess that's why she wanted me to write to her when she got back home. I never did. I didn't need to complicate my present situation. When I left her room I realized that I, and my fingers, had lingered too long. I was supposed to meet Ally for dinner before I went in to do my show, and I was two hours late.

She was suspicious from the get-go. A little inebriated hanky panky with friends as a mutual exercise was one thing, but either of us going off on our own and pulling that shit was a no-no.

"Where were you?" she said.

"Oh, I was over at the pool," I said.

"What were you doing that made you this late?"

I sucked in a breath—a liar's breath—and said, "I met some new friends there. Just some folks down from the states. They were nice. Interesting to talk to. The time ran away with me. I'm sorry."

She glared at me. She knew me. Knew I was lying. I knew I was lying and yet I looked her straight in the eye and gave her that line of bullshit.

"You were with some bitch, weren't you?" she said.

"*Nooo*...it was a mixed group...gals and guys." I could see the hurt in her eyes. I became indignant. "I can have *friends*," I said. There's nothing wrong with *that*."

I went off to work. Nothing was said about it the next day. It was late in the morning and we were still in bed. Ally had her Masque of Tragedy on. Nobody did Little Miss Tragedy better than her. But she said, "Do you want me to fuck you?"

"Yuh," I said.

She sat astride me. Ally loved being on top. I loved her being on top. But this time she wouldn't look at me. Her wistful eyes gazed into some imaginary distance. I was turned on nonetheless.

After a couple minutes she said, "Did you come?"

"Yuh," I muttered.

And with that she dismounted faster than a gymnast off a pommel horse. No tenderness at all. She wanted to be as cold as possible. She was making her point. It was her way of showing me that I was beneath her contempt. A bastard of the first magnitude.

But bastards still get laid.

# Chapter 39

## *BUS STOP*

I liked to take the bus into *Viejo San Juan*. The place where it was all happening. The narrow crowded streets…the smell of greasy food in the air...bars with go-go dancers in elevated cages...atmosphere, man! I could pick the bus up right outside the Borinquen Hotel and it was a straight shot into the old city from there.

The bus rides were an adventure in themselves. One day this homeless looking guy got on and immediately started haranguing the driver. He was in the bus pilot's face, cussing up a blue streak. I couldn't make out everything he was saying in Spanish, but I could pick up on many of the choice words and phrases. The Dude was whacked. The harassment went on for about five minutes, until finally the driver pulled to the side of the road. The bus lurched to a halt. The driver, a man of no insignificant girth, got out of his seat and began going toe to toe with the berserko passenger. It was like one of those baseball games where the team manager is arguing with the umpire...their faces inches from each other and the spittle flying.

The driver ordered the man off the bus. The guy wasn't moving. The driver took him by the arm and pushed him toward the door. Mr Crazy wasn't going down without a fight. He grabbed onto each of the two vertical poles just inside the doorway and held on like a drowning man clutching a tree branch. The driver shoved. The man held fast. Drastic measures would need to be employed. The driver stuck his boot right into the small of the man's back and gave a mighty shove. The whack job tumbled head over ass into the street, but came right back up cursing and shaking his fist as the bus moved slowly away. I flashed back to Rosie on the rollaway bed, hanging on for all she was worth. But for what?

    Sometimes it's better just to let go.

\*

I didn't see it coming. I should have. Things were deteriorating between Ally and me. We were sitting up in bed one night, arguing about something. I don't remember what it was. You see, I can remember details about most things that happened way back in the day—but I can't remember what fights were about. That's because they're usually about things that never matter in the long run. Petulance. Ego. Misunderstanding.

    Ally had cut me off sexually for several days running. And that was the underlying cause of whatever we were pretending the argument was about. She might have intended it as a temporary punishment for my past transgressions, and planned to reinstate me when she'd seen I had suffered enough. But I couldn't be sure of that. For all I knew, it might be permanent. Did she expect us to live together as platonic roommates? I tried to engage her in a sensual embrace. She resisted.

    I exploded. "Get the *fuck* out of my bed, then!"

    Man, I regret saying those words. Down through the years,

they have echoed in my ears. She scrambled off the bed. I had given her a ring—just a simple gold band—it wasn't implying an engagement, but it was meant to cement our feelings for each other. We were going to stick together like glue. She wrested the ring off her finger and slammed it against a far wall. It went skittering. I didn't find it until days after she left. I heard her picking up and packing up some things. And then the slam of the door.

I didn't know if and when I'd ever see her again.

# Chapter 40

## *DAMN HIPPIES!*

I knew that I would have to move on. There would be other Allys. Who was I kidding? There would never be another Ally. But there would be Marias and Susans and Marilyns. Probably not a bad trade-off over the long haul. I didn't like places that held bittersweet memories, so I'd vacated the digs on Del Casse and found an apartment in a quiet residential neighborhood. So quiet that you could hear the drip-drip of your neighbor's leaky faucet.

I was strolling along the grounds of El Morro Castle one evening, alone with my thoughts. El Morro was built way back when Puerto Rico was under Spanish rule. It served as a fortress against would be invaders from the sea—including Sir Francis Drake, who tried but got cannonballs blasting holes in his ship in response. With the Atlantic ocean on one side and *Viejo San Juan*, with its modern day onslaught of tourists on the other, it stood as a bridge between the past and the present. And as I strolled my thoughts were somewhere in that foggy mist between what was then and what was now as well. Between what could have been and what had come to pass.

I came upon a band of hippies who had been camping out there several nights in a row. I told you that I was a "hippie," but by the letter of the law that wasn't exactly true. While I looked the part and loved getting high and loved free love, there was one thing that set me apart from these authentic hippie folk I had just encountered. *I worked for a living.* And work was antithetical to everything true hippies stood for. If you had a job you were part of the establishment. You were workin' for The Man! Nonetheless I connected with them on a cosmic level, and as I was about to mosey on a blonde haired guy with locks down to *there* (Give me a head with hair!) pigeonholed me and said that his wife was six months pregnant, and it had become uncomfortable for her under these primitive conditions. I thought about that no-room-at-the-inn thing from the Biblical story, and I said okay. I'll put the two of you up for tonight.

The following night, when I came home from work to my quiet apartment in my oh so quiet neighborhood, the man and his wife were still there and a friend of theirs had joined them. I frowned. Would it be all right if he stayed too...just for one more night? Again I thought about how Mary and Joseph had been turned away because there was no room at the inn. So I said okay.

You know where this is going.

Before long I had a whole houseful of hippies! They were sleeping in my bed, and when I got up (off the floor) to take a piss in the middle of the night, there would be some chick I'd never seen before taking a shower in my bathroom.

Things were starting to get out of hand.

There was this big fuzzy bear of a guy who threw the *I-Ching* every morning, which ostensibly served as his spiritual guidance for what to do, or not to do (most likely the latter) on that particular day. When I'd leave to go to work, they would razz me for having a job. Never considering, I guess, that my gainful employment was what provided the roof that was currently over their heads.

Mrs. Pereira was my landlady. She was such a sweet older lady. And I know she believed I would be the ideal tenant, being who I was and all.

But those damn hippies.

I got a call from Mrs. Pereira, and I knew it had to be something out of the ordinary for her to phone me at work. And her hysterical tone—that was a pretty big clue too. *Mr. Brown...the neighbors call me! The people...the people...they are running NA-KED in the street...and they are coming from your apartment!*

"Whoops...uh, Mrs. Pereira, so sorry...I had no idea. I will put a stop to that. Yes, it's terrible, don't worry..."

But there was no consoling her. Like all nice people, she had her limits. And I felt bad for putting her in the position of having to tell me I would need to find another place to live.

If that doesn't make me a nice guy, I don't know what does.

# Chapter 41

## *SMILING FACES*

I'd re-established residency at the Borinquen Hotel due to circumstances beyond my control. Hoping that everybody would just leave me alone for a while.

What I really needed at the moment was a friend. And as fate would have it, I met a guy named Ramon—who looked like he could have been an Argentinian soccer player, or maybe a Peruvian fish monger. He could have been a lot of things except who and what he initially tried to pass himself off to me as, and that was Daniel Lugo—a popular Spanish language television soap opera star of the day. Not being a fan of soap operas (except my own), I had never seen Daniel Lugo, so I took my new friend at his word. He seemed like an affable sort, and I still wanted to believe in people—give everyone the benefit of the doubt (a major character flaw of mine that has taken decades to pummel into submission).

I did find it strange, though, that "Daniel Lugo" would want to camp out on the floor of my apartment for a couple nights. He said he was conducting some business in that part of town, and it would be more convenient for him than going back and forth from his home, wherever that was. He didn't strike me as the type who would go running naked through the hotel lobby, so I shrugged and told him he could stay the couple nights, which, you guessed it, turned into a few more than that. During that time he admitted that he was not Mr. Lugo—he was only kidding about that, ha ha. That initial deception was something I should have paid more attention to though, considering how things would shake out in the end.

But it was good to have a friend, and we'd hang out together—sometimes just go joy riding in his car. He'd spot a girl on the street, stop the car and get out, intercept her and start in with a line of bullshit: *Mama you look so fine...I'd like to get to know you*...on and on. He had the looks to be on TV, so oftentimes the woman would appear to be flattered—at least she would entertain what he had to say. Until he'd come up with: *Yo quiero chichar contigo!* Asking her point blank if she wanted to fuck. Puerto Rican women wouldn't kick you in the balls, or fire off a barrage of muthafucka this and muthafucka that—they'd just turn in a huff and walk away with their heads held high, refusing to waste another second of their precious time on a scum sucking pig such as yourself.

Then came the day when we were off to somewhere—Ramon behind the wheel and me riding shotgun. There was a young guy—looked like an American tourist—on the right hand sidewalk coming toward us. Ramon swerved onto the walkway and took dead aim at the kid, who at first didn't react, thinking that no one in their right mind (and that was the key) was going to try to randomly run him down here in a decent neighborhood of San

Juan (not good for tourism).That quickly changed to the terror I saw in his eyes as he realized the vehicle was headed straight toward him and wasn't going to veer (and I'm thinking Ramon wants to scare the guy—an asshole thing to do—but he had a quirky sense of humor). The kid leaped out of the way at the last second, slamming against the doorway of a nearby edifice. Ramon had no intention of merely scaring him. He would have hit the kid and taken off. Laughing.

Attempted murder.

I said to myself, well...this guy can't be staying at my place anymore.

*

I told Ramon that he was cramping my style and that he would have to go home. I'd be having some chicks over, ya know? (that was wishful thinking at this point). No problem, he said. Earlier that morning he had shaken me awake at the ungodly hour of 7am. He said that he had run into a female fan of mine in the lobby, and he'd promised he could get my autograph for her.

"Wha?" I said. My head was real fuzzy at that hour.

"Come on...do a young girl a favor. It will make her happy." He produced a pen and a pad of paper. "Here, just sign this."

I started to write C-H-A-R—but he said no, I should sign my real name. It would be more authentic. What the hell. I scribbled it out.

"Is that the way you always write it?" he queried.

"Yeah, sure."

"Thanks, man. You gonna make her real happy."

I thought, whatever, and went back to Snoozeville.

\*

I was cavalier about money. It was my hippie mentality. As long as I had a roof and a nice plate of rice and beans in front of me I was good. I'd typically have two or three paychecks sitting in my mail slot at work. Uncashed. Undeposited. There were checks piling up at the ad agency where I did some freelance commercial work. I was too lazy to go and pick them up. And I left my checkbook lying around in plain sight on the table at my apartment. I know what you're thinking. HOW AMAZINGLY...INCREDIBLY... STUPENDOUSLY STUPID WAS THAT?

Well, you're about to find out.

\*

Davey O'Donnell was a Louisiana boy who had recently joined the WBMJ jock lineup. He had an elfin kind of charm and an infectious smile. Folks were easily drawn into his orbit, and there was usually something doing at his place. Getting high, laughing, passing out and waking with the first slant of sun in the morning. Stumbling out the door and making your way home.

One night after work I dropped by Davey's place at his invitation. Ramon had weaseled his way into Davey's good graces as well, and I found him and my radio cohort in the kitchen. "Charlie, have a beer," said Davey, grinning like he was running for office. Someone tapped me on the shoulder from behind. I turned. It was a naked Puerto Rican chick with orange hair. Solidly constructed, but I could easily see that orange was not her natural hair color. She gave me a hug. I recognized her as the one who came to the radio station with Ramon one day and asked if I would slip my hand up her dress. I felt embarrassed to be doing that. I never cared for women who were so blatantly sexual that they were pushy about it. I liked whores, but I wasn't fond of sluts, I guess you could say.

Angie was her name. "Come on, let's go," she said. I assumed that both Davey and Ramon had had her, and now it was my turn. She pulled me into the bedroom and as soon as we hit the sheets I could tell that my heart wasn't in it. The lights were on. The door was open. I expected Davey and Ramon to come in at any moment to see how I was doing. Maybe shout a few words of encouragement.

There's a dud in every pack of firecrackers. And tonight I was that dud. It was embarrassing, but I wasn't prone to performing in the absence of a modicum of affection—something that builds for say, three months, or three days, or three hours—but hardly in a span of three minutes.

Fortunately, they didn't come in. I made some excuse about wanting to go to the kitchen for water. Ramon told me that she wanted to stay with me. Take her home with you and you can do her all night.

Right.

I took Angie back to my pad at the hotel. Never say die. We got into bed. But her mood had turned. I got a nice view of her back as she studied the wall. The sudden bitchiness piqued my interest. There was no challenge before, but now...

She feigned sleep. But she wasn't getting off that easy. I was beginning to respond. Somebody down there liked me! I seized the moment and slid into her from the pooch position, with The Doors "Back Door Man" playing in my head. She was cold as leftover pizza, so I concentrated on my own pleasure. It was over quickly—a whimpering little fuck, but I had triumphed nonetheless. She rose, still pouting, and retreated to the other room, dragging my sheet and blanket along with her. Let her stay out there. I don't give a damn.

I was ready to rack up some REMs when I heard a loud rap rap rap upon my door. Goddamn, it's three o'clock in the morning! I stumbled out of bed, pussyfooting my way through the darkened living room. "Who the hell is it?"

"It's *Bella*," said the voice from the other side of the world. My luck with the ladies had recently picked up, and Bella was a product of that good fortune.

I knew that I was in trouble. I opened the door, grasped Bella's hand and led her into the bedroom, hoping that she wouldn't notice any orange colored lumps lying on the living room floor—or worse, that she should stumble over one.

"Sooo...what's new?" I said. "*Man,* I sure am sleepy." But

Bella, good ol' acid-head Bella—lithe, brown, beach goddess, disco queen Bella, who was evolved beyond her eons and knew exactly what she wanted, was in no mood for my coyness.

"CHARLIE—I WANT TO FUCK!" she proclaimed to the universe as she hiked up her skirt.

My anxiety returned. It was short notice for any kind of repeat performance. My flagging member was at half mast, but she uttered some kind of incantation and before you knew it I was standing at attention again—the proud symbol of American manhood!

She lowered herself onto me, and I was thankful that she was prepared to do all the work. She moaned. She snorted. She growled. She whinnied. And in the throes of her orgasm, she invoked the names of every deity of the world's major and minor religions.

And I'm saying GO BABY GO while simultaneously thinking: *Hear that, bitch in the other room? You'd have to be Helen Keller not to hear that! NOW you understand, you slut...now you understand!*

# Chapter 42

## *TROJAN HORSE*

A week or so later I stopped by my bank to draw some spending money out of my checking account. The teller politely informed me that the hundred dollar check I had made out to "cash" would bounce because I only had five dollars and change in my account. My jaw dropped to the floor. There had been plenty of money in that account and I knew that I hadn't withdrawn essentially all of it. And then it hit me like a rotten tomato upside the head, dribbling down my face in seeds of meaning.

*Ramon!*

*Do you always sign your name this way?* It had been early in the morning with my head in a purple haze when he asked me that. And I'd just shrugged it off.

I demanded to see the bank manager, who shall heretofore be referred to by the initials of "B.M." I explained the situation to him. Mr. B.M. excused himself and came back with a printout of several checks that had cleared, some made out to local businesses, with my signature down at the bottom. Except they weren't a very good forgery of my name. Then Mr B.M. threw in the clincher. "I remember seeing you in here last week," he said.

What? Was I going crazy? I knew that I hadn't set foot in that bank for at least a month, and I knew those were not my signatures on those checks. The bank had screwed up. Mr B.M. sensed that it could reflect badly upon him, and he was trying to cover his ass.

The plot thickens.

*

I was lounging at the pool when these two FBI guys (I'm assuming that's who they were) came to collect me. They certainly looked the part with their suits and dark sunglasses. They said, "Let's go for a little ride."

They hauled me around to visit some local merchants where some of those checks had been used to purchase crap. They wanted the merchants to identify me as the guy, or not the guy, who made those purchases. Just to see if Charlie Brown was telling the truth. That seemed reasonable, but it made me extremely nervous. What if one of those merchants looked at me and said yeah, he's the guy, just like the bank manager had claimed he'd spotted me at the bank when I wasn't there? At this point, I wasn't sure if I could trust *anybody*.

Fortunately, each of those store folk looked at me, scowled, and shook their heads. No, he's not the one. Now there was proof that I'd been ripped off—to the tune of what would be roughly nine thousand dollars in today's funds.

Ramon had hatched a truly diabolical plot to repay me for my kindness to him. He got me to take Angie home with me that night. She was the one who removed blank checks—out of the middle of the sheaf in my checkbook—so I wouldn't notice them missing right away (all while I was "entertaining" Bella). That way Ramon wouldn't be implicated (or so he thought) in the theft. Angie delivered the checks to Ramon and he took it from there, no doubt giving her a cut of the action for a job well done. Because Angie was nowhere to be found. It was apparent that she had skipped the island and absconded, mostly likely to New York. But Ramon was still around, and the authorities were familiar with my psychopathic friend. And here's the kicker. Ramon's father was a JUDGE! No wonder he thought he could get away with murder, or just about anything else.

Ramon was charged, however, and I agreed to testify at his trial. I was sitting in a room next to the courtroom, waiting for them to call me in. Then someone came and told me that the trial had been put off. Postponed or canceled, I didn't know which. Did Ramon cop a plea, or did his influential father pull some strings to get him off? I figured it was the latter, because I never heard anything more about it...

I got all my money back in the end. And the bank manager got demoted for maintaining his bullshit story about me. I began to think that maybe there was some justice in the world after all. But then I still believed, as a lot of us did back then, that we could change the world into a place where love prevailed, and greed and avarice would no longer dictate the terms of nearly everything.

# Chapter 43

## *RUBBER BALL (BOUNCY BOUNCY!)*

Whenever I was on the rebound I didn't think so clearly. My existential angst would have me calling out: *Next woman up!* And because of the times and because of being in the public eye, I had ample opportunity for one night stands, or single week whirlwind affairs with strangers on their island getaway. But at heart I was a relationship guy. I wanted someone to be there when I came home from work—someone I wouldn't have to ask what her name was when I woke up beside her in the morning.

And so I thought of Susan. It had been three years. I let her dump me off at the Newport Beach bus station after we had run out of road on our Latin American odyssey. I think I had written her a couple of "friendly" letters since, just so as not to lose touch. We had been such a great fit. Why hadn't I followed up on it? Because she had her life in California and I had mine in the midwest? I put pen to paper and told her what I was thinking (in my addled brain). I told her there'd been no one else (Ally notwithstanding) that I would seriously consider marrying other than her, and what would she think about a couple weeks all expenses paid vacation to sunny Puerto Rico? I sent the letter off on an adrenaline high, hoping that she'd still be at the same address.

We'd met at a border crossing in Honduras. I was on a devil-may-care road trip adventure with three of my buddies from

Iowa—through Mexico and central America and wherever we ended up. Susan and her traveling companion, Louie, exchanged pleasantries with us and well wishes for a safe journey.

The next time I saw her was in Panama. As you've already seen, serendipity has played a major role in my life. Susan and Louie were staying at the Hotel Ideal—same as me and my pals in Panama City! We all met up for dinner and later on she would tell me that I must have had some upbringing because I held my knife and fork continental style (actually it was because I was a southpaw).

Susan was hip and witty, with a southern California cosmopolitan air about her. Once I'd learned that her companion Louie was just a friend, I began spending some time with her. It was monsoon season. Every day the rains came, and we followed suit. Then she told me that she and Louie were going to start heading back north...and was I coming? Geez, well...I've got my buddies here. I wouldn't want to cut out on them.

In the end I cut out on them. Left them a note. *A damn note!* Susan, Louie and I headed out in her green Volkswagen Beetle that had been dubbed "The Pukemobile." We'd made it up to Managua, Nicaragua when Louie started feeling like a third wheel. He'd likely had some undeclared designs on his traveling companion himself, but saw the writing on the wall. He told us that he was going to head out on his own. He was Hispanic, and thought he could make his way around okay. That left me and Susan.

Two for the road.

We drove up through the Yucatan and took a boat out to *Isla Mujeres*—an unspoiled, magical little island. It was like going back in time. And for us, time stood still. We saw stardust dripping from our fingers in the bioluminescent bay. We were in lust, in a tropical paradise.

And then came Mexico City. The Beetle had stalled in the middle of traffic. Couldn't get it started again. Clueless and hapless looking, we stood around saying "well shit, what do we do now?" A nice bespectacled man stopped to help us. He made an expert assessment. "You are out of gas, my friends!" Hmmm...why hadn't we thought of that?.

He drove me to a Pemex station while Susan stayed with the car. We returned with a container full of *gasolina*, fed it to the thirsty bug and started 'er up.

His name was Roberto. A veterinarian by trade. A good Samaritan veterinarian! We thanked him profusely—offered some pesos which he refused—and went on our way. Roberto had given us his business card, and that evening Susan said you know we should invite him to have a drink with us tonight. I said I thought that might be carrying things a bit far. Because Susan, with her longish blonde hair and blue eyes, was something of a rarity down here. A goddess, perhaps, in the eyes of many of the men. But she coaxed me into it. We really should thank the man properly, after all.

Roberto picked us up at our hotel and took us to a local cantina, where the booze and the mariachi music were flowing freely. "Drink up, my friends!" he said. And why not, he was buying. The remainder of the evening proceeded in "poetic" fashion:

Their gracious host
The Good Samaritan Veterinarian
grabs the gringa
and bolts for the door of the cantina.

A mad dash
and a merry chase
across a Mexico City park ensues.

Farm Boy
who has only an hour's familiarity
with the healing properties of tequila
sensing that shortly
it will purge his system
is now playing catch up.

Should have seen it coming
down here
with that hair
those eyes
and her white Levis.

Back at the "Pukemobile"
(it ain't easy bein' green)
all are polite
in the gilded night.

The doc generously offers to drive
in fits and starts
down dead-end streets
back tracking
plowing over road signs
and in the back
laying low
Farm Boy narrowly avoids

the blow back of his paramour's barf
out the open window
into the warm breeze
of a tropical night
(the old Beetle living up to its handle at last).

At the hotel
two boys on the steps
look quizzically at the little entourage
as Boy volunteers *"Borracho"*
by way of explanation
They shake their heads knowingly
already familiar
in their tender years
with the spectacle
of shit-faced gringos
bouncing off the walls
with lecherous Latinos
in hot pursuit.

Regrouped sufficiently now
to wonder
can they reach the room in time
to ditch the doc
but his foot wedged
inside the door
brings the promise of more.

Boy hangs on desperately
to the bed
as the room spins
like a carnival ride.

You are sick my friends
Samaritan says
(another debt of gratitude they owe—
the animal doctor has diagnosed them for free!)
providing wet towels
for their heads.

There is a lull in the action.

Then...
Squirming
kicking
biting
cussing
and disparaging his ancestry
Blondie's jeans
are down
around
her ankles
the bespectacled
man of medicine
lowering himself onto her...

But access to the moving target
is denied.

A momentary stalemate
as in the spaghetti westerns
right before the *climactic* scene...

(Boy's passivity stems not only
from an inability to discern up from down
but out of a morbid curiosity
to see how she will handle it—
having invited the "nice man" for a drink
against Boy's better judgment).

The question becomes moot
as the doc
feeling he's beat
appears to be heading for the door
but not before
he takes matters into his own hand
and stops to fire a parting shot
across the bow
his aim true
strafing the both of them with his seed
as they lie there
too pathetic

and stupefied
to care.

\*

Susan's reply arrived in the mail. Whenever I would open a letter from a woman, I'd take a deep breath. Because it could only be one of two things. Good news or bad news. *Ahhh*...she was intrigued by the prospect of visiting me! And the things I had written regarding my previously unstated feelings for her. We talked by phone, shoring up the details and the logistics of how this thing would work. And then the day arrived.

A warm embrace at the airport. She was lovely. But she was awfully thin. I didn't know anything about anorexia at the time. I just figured she had an obsession about not gaining weight (which, in simplified terms, is what anorexia is about). She'd never had a weight problem that I was aware of. But as I would learn, it was more about a distorted body image in one's mind.

But she still looked hot in that black dress! I showed her—and showed her off—to my San Juan. I didn't take her to the cheap curbside food places (that I might have frequented otherwise). I took her to the Caribe Hilton for dinner and drinks. We'd have languid intellectual conversations. She could talk to you on your level—politics, religion, philosophy, whatever. I knew I'd made a good choice in bringing her here.

In bed, she was hesitant. It had been a long time between times for us, and for her to get back into that mindset would take more than the flip of a switch. It took reassurances from me that it wasn't just about physical sex. I was patient and gentle. But one day she came out with it. "I get the feeling that maybe I'm just a sex object for you." She needed a serious straightening out.

"Listen," I said. "I have plenty of opportunity around here for that sort of thing. Why would I bring *you* all the way out here from California if that's all I wanted? I could have gotten off a lot cheaper by just going across the street to the Black Angus cathouse!"

That seemed to ease her mind, and our lovemaking got better. And then it was time for her to go back. Three years ago at the bus station all she'd said was "I don't like goodbyes, so…" And then she was gone. It was a warmer farewell this time, because we had discussed making our relationship into a permanent thing. She would go back and get her shit together. I would get my shit together, and when we both had our shit together, she would come back and we would be together.

# Chapter 44

## *FLASHBACK: IT'S FUN TO STAY AT THE Y.M.C.A.*

1963. The die had been cast. My direction set at last. I was enrolled in a radio and television broadcasting school in Chicago—operated by legendary New York City radio and TV personality Fred Robbins (Robbins is credited as being the first prominent jazz disc-jockey!). Myself and a few other colorful individuals from around the country had come to learn the basics of our chosen craft. Yes, it was so obvious now. Why hadn't I seen it when I first strapped that little radio onto the handlebars of my bike?

Midwestern Broadcasting School. It was kind of a Julliard for disc-jockeys. And when we weren't practicing how to cue up a record, read a commercial, or learn the proper pronunciation of *Hors de Oeuvres*, there was free time to fill. I was residing at the YMCA Hotel on south Wabash Avenue. It was cheap, but you couldn't exactly call it student housing. Nearly every day I'd get hit on by homosexuals. It didn't bother me that much—in fact I was flattered. It just wasn't my preference. (But the impressions you picked up from The Village People's recording of "YMCA" were spot on.)

Ah, but here was something the whole family could enjoy. Music! They were looking for someone to host the regular Saturday night record hop down in the rec room. I applied for it, and because I was a broadcasting student, I got the gig. We are gonna have some fun now!

It became a popular event. Straight folk, gay folk, and lots of black folk would come out to boogie the night away. The song I got the most requests for was "Shake A Tail Feather" by The Five Du-Tones. There was some serious dancin' going on to that song, It was a hot number (it requests repeatedly that you bend over), and many of those folks would have looked right at home on *Soul Train* when it debuted eight years later in 1971.

There was a B-side to each one of those 45s I was slapping onto my hot, hard-working turntable, and one night I got curious and started flipping some of the records over to hear what was on the other side. It was a real musical grab bag—some of the songs weren't bad, I thought, some of 'em were kind of crappy. But it put a real damper on the dancing because people didn't recognize the songs. Most of them were sitting around wondering what the hell I was doing.

A big, menacing looking dude came up to the bandstand and said, "WHO IS PLAYIN' ALL DA BULLSHIT?" I had another young guy up there with me who was acting as my assistant to find records that had been requested, and he immediately stepped away from me and said, "I not playin' da bullshit." Some friend he was, eh?"

I NOT PLAYIN' DA BULLSHIT!

Well, that left only one individual in the place who could have possibly been playin' da bullshit...and it was, of course, Yours

Truly. Needless to say, with that nasty looking dude staring menacingly at me, I quickly got us back on track with the music and everyone hit the dance floor again.

Lesson learned: the customer is always right. Especially when he looks mean and might have a blade tucked inside his shoe.

# Chapter 45

## *LOOK SHARP, BE SHARP*

James Brown was coming to Puerto Rico for an outdoor concert at Hiram Bithorn Stadium, and I had to see him. This wasn't going to be like The Rascals (formerly The Young Rascals) concert which I had emceed—standing up on stage flashing the peace sign to adoring fans, getting carried away and removing my sandals and flinging them into the crowd where there was a mad scramble and somebody either wore those smelly things home, or had them bronzed and placed upon the mantle next to their baby shoes. I was going to see James Brown as a fan, and boogie like a sex machine.

    I arrived at the stadium early. You could either sit in the stands or go out onto the field and get closer to the stage, and that's what I planned to do. As I came through the admittance gate, there were a couple people handing out samples of razor blades as a promotional gimmick. Pick up your razor blades, take 'em home and try them on your beard, or if you were female you could test them on your legs...or maybe your bush (whoops, we were still in the days when most women didn't defoliate. I still prefer a little decorative shrubbery down there to the starkly barren landscape that's in vogue these days). I pocketed my shaving accessories and went to find a good spot near the stage.

    James Brown—Soul Brother Number One—was putting on a

show, doing his acrobatic moves and belting out some of his great hits such as "I Got You," and "Papa's Got A Brand New Bag." I was in the front row of fans and digging it. But who knows what malevolent forces can seize upon a gathering where music would normally bring everyone together? They were present on that night.

Out of the blue, a beer bottle was lobbed upon the stage. The Godfather Of Soul paid it no mind. Another bottle was hurled, missing the performer but coming close. James Brown, the ultimate showman, kept on doing his thing. But now the stage was being pelted with miscellaneous crap.

All the lights went out. The stadium was plunged into total darkness. An ominous murmur welled up from the crowd. The concert was over half way through. Some of the lights came back on and that's when I began to hear screams. Some people were rushing toward me. "RUN!" I heard one of them say. "They're cutting people up with razor blades!" A sick feeling hit me in the pit of my stomach. Some "enterprising" thugs had opened their packages of blades and were moving through the crowd slashing people. The scene erupted into chaos as fans began to catch on to what was going down. Some climbed the wire mesh fence behind the home plate area, hanging on for dear life. I tried to fight my way toward the exit, but it was hard. I saw a man with blood on his face and on his arms. "STUPID FUCKERS!" I shouted. Who gives away razor blades to thousands of people gathered in one place? Some of those people are bound to be sick fucks!

It was sheer terror. One of those grisly slasher movies come to life on a grand scale. I wondered if the next person I encountered would be coming at me, ready to slash my face open. I fought through the crowd like a salmon swimming upstream. The exit was up ahead. Instinctively, I reached behind me to see if another hand wanted to grab onto mine. One did...I didn't know if it was a man or a woman. All I can tell you is that angels (maybe the same ones who were present in Curacao) guided us the rest of the way.

I don't remember seeing much of anything about it in the San Juan Star the next day. It should have been a major story. In preparation for writing this memoir, I scoured the internet trying to find any trace of that James Brown concert in San Juan. It seems to have disappeared into the murky haze of forgotten history. Perhaps because it was in the best interest of so many who were connected to it to let it remain that way.

# Chapter 46

## *EBONY AND IVORY*

It had been a few weeks and I got a call from Susan. It was the first crack in the veneer. She started off with "So what's going on? Where are we?" I assured her that I was formulating my plan for us and I would get back to her on that. But I had no plan. I was just moving things to the back burner because the more time I had to think about it, the more the reality of the situation began to sink in. We were gonna get *married*, man! The only thing I had to compare the word marriage to was my parents own dysfunctional, booze-driven debacle. More time, I told myself. I needed more time to think this thing out. I was hoping Susan would understand.

\*

Some of the smaller FM outlets (AM radio was still king) were following WBMJ's lead and began playing some American pop/rock. There was a black dude named Tony doing an airshift on one of them, and he called me up one day just to say hi and let me know that he was a fan. He was fairly new to the business and said he liked to listen to me to see "how it was done." Really nice guy. I invited him to visit me at the station and we became fast friends. Tony had an afro and in person he was a jive-talker. But he didn't sound black on the radio. The ongoing goof between the two of us was that his listeners thought he was white, and a lot of mine thought I was black.

Tony had to move out of his current digs and was looking for a place to hang his hat. I thought of Mary and Joseph and no room at the inn (again!) and told him he could share my pad. I had moved to a spacious apartment on Loiza Street, a little funkier neighborhood than my previous residences. We took stock of the place and thought of what we could do to personalize it—make it more reflective of who we were. We got two buckets of paint, black and white, and redid that entire place—bedrooms, living room, bathroom, kitchen—in alternating zebra stripes of black and white! (without the landlord's permission). With bold strokes, we simultaneously expressed our unity and our diversity. People were knocked out by it.

One day I came across Tony lending a sympathetic ear to a diminutive Puerto Rican chick name Maria at the pool bar. She was bemoaning the fact that her boyfriend was such a shit. And now he wasn't even coming around. I politely asked if I could join them and it was cool. As Maria went on, describing this guy, I realized that she had sold herself short. She was a cute girl and she deserved better. Tony knew her from before, and I could see that he was trying to console her, not hit on her. When he had to leave for work. I stuck around and continued to provide a sympathetic ear.

"Listen," I said. "This guy has got you down. I hate to see you go home this way. Why don't we go take a walk." And with that she started to perk up.

"Back there you said you were feeling lonely and blue," I said.

"Yeah," she said.

"Well, Maybe we can do something about that."

As the words left my mouth, I had Susan on my mind and I felt guilty. But not too guilty not to provide a lonely girl with some companionship.

*

Maria and I started hanging out together in the way that people do. You know, when they are out and about they are wearing some nice clothes—and when they are alone together, they're not wearing any clothes.

Tony, on the other hand, seemed to be on a losing streak. I saw him strike out with beautiful black girls on numerous occasions. He couldn't figure it out. I told him you gotta make a new plan, man! And so he came to do better with white chicks. Conversely, I had been making out pretty well with women of color. There was none of this "he should be with his own kind and I should be with my own kind" among the beautiful people of the sixties and seventies. That only existed with the older generation, and probably more so with conservative Puerto Rican families.

That's why it was such a kick for Tony, Maria, and me to hang out. We'd walk down the street together, three abreast. Tony, the dark roast cup of java on one end. Me, the vanilla milkshake on the other. Maria, a lovely mocha shaded blend of the two of us in the middle. Black. White. Puerto Rican. We were a prism of light and love, and we got some interesting looks from folks as we passed by. I can tell you that I was never prouder of who I was—of who we were—than during those moments.

*

I'll bet you have one moment—one *special* moment from the past where you literally or figuratively were rolling on the floor...busting a gut at something somebody said or did. And when you think about it today, it still has the power to make you spew your drink all over your nice new shirt. I'm going to relate to you what that moment was for me, with the disclaimer that "you had to be there," and you need a certain depraved sense of humor to appreciate it (and since you've gotten this far in the book, I'm assuming you do).

Tony had dug up this Italian girl from the Bronx (I shouldn't say dug up because she wasn't a zombie, though she may be one by now). I'm going to call her Sofia. It was good to see Tony with someone, and I suggested that the four of us—Maria and me, and Tony and Sofia—go out on a double date.

We went to a movie, a forgettable one. All I remember is that it wasn't *Balls In Action*. There were a couple of skin flick theaters in town, and the one I rode by on the bus a lot had BALLS IN ACTION in big bold lettering up on the marquee for the longest time. It seemed like months. I never saw it, but it must have been a classic to be held over for that long (I've just added it to my bucket list, if the film might ever be located at this point).

After the movie we popped into one of the Condado hotels.

We had some wine. We had some laughs. It was plain to see that Sofia was sweet on Tony—she was hanging on him all evening long. Afterward, we dropped her off in my UFO. That stood for "Used Fucked Opal." Which is what I would say when anybody would ask what make of car it was. It wasn't a real looker, but it ran.

Tony helped Sofia out of the car, and she clung to him like Saran Wrap on a half-eaten sticky bun. Tony got back into the car. She stuck her head through the open window and, dreamy-eyed, she said, "Goodnight, darling!" Now, you have to understand that Tony spoke the way he spoke. It was ghetto talk. And he wasn't going to alter it to suit your gender, race, or religion. With Tony, it was one size fits all. So when Sofia came out with her *goodnight darling*, Tony looked at her—just as deadpan as could be—and said, "G'NIGHT MOTHERFUCKER." Oh...the look...the look on her face as we drove away! I'm guffawing again as I write this.

Like I said, you had to be there.

*

Susan called me one more time. She essentially told me to put up or shut up...but make up your damn mind! I think she knew which direction it was going. Here's where I bring in all the old cliches: *Out of sight, out of mind...A bird in the hand...*

I had a bird, Maria, and she was singing sweetly to me. Susan was out there in the bush somewhere in California. Long distance relationships are so tough. Especially when you've placed your trust in an erratic young guy (me) who was, let's face it, a lothario.

I never called Susan again and she never called me. I couldn't just come out and say it! I was always riding the fence, trying to keep my options open. That's what an opportunist does. Susan deserved better. A lot better than to be dumped in such a disdainful manner by a callous bastard like me. If I could go back there now, I'd slap the shit out of myself.

# Chapter 47

## *I READ THE NEWS TODAY, OH BOY*

I was getting my own TV show! Dean, the General Manager at WTSJ-TV, channel 18, San Juan's only English language station, had talked to me about it. What a cool thing, to have Charlie Brown doing what essentially would be a radio deejay show on the boob tube, eh? I could pretty much do what I wanted with it. That was his first mistake. We were going to do the show live. That was his second mistake.

I thought, hey, I'll get me some sexy lookin' chicks and they'll dance to the songs I play. What could go wrong? I was in wing-it mode. Arrogant. Overconfident. Now, you can do a radio show by winging it, and that's basically what I did every day. But I had plenty of experience in radio. You can write a memoir by winging it, and that's kind of what we're doing here, kids. My writing style doesn't lend itself to having much of an outline because the narrative can shoot off in unexpected directions. That's the fun and the beauty of writing. But you should never go into a medium you are unfamiliar with and think you can wing it.

I called the show *Boogie Street*. On the kickoff we went live and it was going well at first. I had recruited some dark-haired, exotic looking lovelies who were willing to dance for the exposure, and they were movin' and groovin' to my first song. Then the camera trained on me and I did a short opening bit and said let's get back to music. That's where it all went into the dumper. We were still using those old cartridge tapes for playing commercials on the radio (they look kinda like 8-tracks, for those who are unfamiliar), and the music was spun on the turntables. There were no turntables at the TV studio, so I transferred some songs onto "cart" and was going to play them off of there. I pressed the button on the cart machine and...the tape jammed. I pulled the plastic cart out of the player and held it up to the camera. The tape was dangling out the ass end, all twisted up. Funny, right? No problem. I stuck a different cart into the machine and...nothing. It had jammed also. And there went my music, and with it the whole concept of the show.

I lost it. Went into panic mode—and it showed. There was a guy there I had standing by as a guest if I needed him—he was a sculptor and had brought along some of his works. I quickly brought him on and he started showing off his pieces. I wasn't listening to what he was saying. I was seething. When he was finished, that was it. The show was cut short because there was nowhere to go with it after that. I had been the victim of technology, or the lack of it. How simple it would have been with the touch computer screens of today. Touch the screen and play the song.

I laid low all the rest of that week. Didn't want to listen to any disparaging comments from people about the show. We actually did a second episode the next weekend, and it went better. But the deejay concept got scrapped. The show didn't know what it was at that point. It had no identity. Mercifully, Dean pulled the plug on it. Video had killed the radio star.

But not for long.

*

I wasn't going to throw in the towel. I'd survived too much shit in my life and come out on top in the end. I was going to master this medium one way or the other.

So I reinvented myself. As a newsman.

Dean liked me, and still wanted to find a place for me at the station. I had gone back to doing daytime shifts on WBMJ, so that opened it up for me to become the 10pm TV news anchor. Quite a switch in image from wacky Charlie Brown on the radio. Along with that, I was going to learn every phase of a TV station's operation. Make myself that versatile and valuable guy who could step into any role at a moment's notice. I did camera work, film editing, sitting in the catbird seat and running things from inside the control room, and helped to produce some of the local shows that we originated.

For the news, I put on a coat and tie (of all the heinous things) and became that authoritative presence that would come into your living room each evening. The dressing up part of it I considered a goof. I was a hippie at heart and always would be. In between the radio and the TV gigs, I'd often relax at the pool. When I got "dressed up" to go on camera, I was still wearing my swim trunks and sandals. I simply donned the jacket and tie over that, and went into work that way. The viewers could see me from the waist up only, and had no idea of my creative mix and match attire, and that I was essentially wearing "no pants."

I didn't play it completely straight on the news. I would do subtle little WTF things. Sometimes I'd have this cigar burning in an ashtray next to me. I'd wrap up the news with a straight face, take a big puff off the cigar, and blow the smoke into the camera. Just a little something to get folks to say: *Hmm...he's an odd duck, isn't he?*

Another time I wanted to make a subtle statement—editorialize, if you will—but slip it right past the "squares." I had a news item about a sewer main bursting and spewing shit all over, and I decided to flash some combat images of the Vietnam War along with the story. I don't suppose too many folks got it. Especially not the flamingly gay guy who called me right after I'd signed off. He was having a hissy fit. "Your photos did not match the story you were reading," he said indignantly. "Another example of INCORRIGIBLE INCOMPETENCE!" He said it with such smugness, such superiority in his rightness—that I had to laugh (and don't we all find ourselves in his shoes from time to time? So sure of ourselves when we really don't have a fucking clue). But I love that phrase...*incorrigible incompetence*...it rolls off the tongue so beautifully. I've used it numerous times over the years when the occasion called for it...*begged* for it...and now I bequeath it to you. Use only as directed.

\*

Celebrities were always popping in and out of the Channel 18 studios, dropping by to do interviews in conjunction with their appearances at the major San Juan hotels. Phyllis Diller came in right after she got her nose job. She looked good! (I went back and forth on whether I should hit on her). It must have been a tough decision to get rid of the one thing—her prominent proboscis—that she had bounced so many one liners off of in her comedy routines.

Nina van Pallandt—who appeared with Richard Gere in *American Gigolo*, and several Robert Altman films—was another captivating figure who graced our studios. I recall her sitting pensively on some wooden bleachers there in the studio, waiting for her turn to go on.

The bleachers were there because of this guy who called himself Eddie Spaghetti. He was a Buffalo Bob type who would herd in about thirty to forty little kids—ages five to eight—providing a kind of poor man's Peanut Gallery as they sat and fidgeted on those bleachers. He was a zany figure who did a weekly show where he would tell some silly jokes, and then try to get all the kids to do a sing-along in unison, which was no easy feat. I don't know where he got all the little ones every week. I've no doubt he lurked outside elementary schools and abducted many of them.

Baron De Beer was a local curmudgeonly type. He played the British Ambassador in Woody Allen's *Bananas*, much of which was filmed in Old San Juan. On his TV show he would sit behind a desk and rattle on and on about something or other. He'd ask me for feedback and I'd tell him what I thought worked and what didn't.

A Miss Universe came by—don't remember which one offhand—but needless to say she was pleasing to the eye. I was operating the camera for her interview, and I may have inadvertently panned slowly up and down her body a couple of times when I should have stayed keyed in on her face. The story of my life. If only I could have stayed focused on higher things.

The Miss Universe I do remember fondly was Marisol Malaret from Puerto Rico, who won the crown in 1970. My connection to Marisol went like this: one of the jocks at the radio station told me that he had fielded a call from a girl who was inquiring about me. She told him to pass along to me that she wanted to—how shall I put this—engage in an act of oral stimulation upon my person. Well, that's interesting, I thought, since she indicated that I should expect to see her up at Penthouse One in the near future. I kept that in the back of my mind for a couple of weeks and then one night there she was, as promised. I feel an excerpt from a poem coming on:

You took the elevator
Up to Penthouse One at the station
I slapped on the long version of In-A-Gadda-Da-Vida
And stood monitoring its progress
Through the plate glass window
As you got into the groove
And did what you said you'd do over the phone
On your knees there on the roof garden

The lights of San Juan shimmering around us.
When your girlfriend came outside
I flinched
You didn't miss a beat.

Her name was Paloma. Dusky. Hair as dark as midnight. As I would learn later, after she'd established a regular regimen of overnight weekend stays at my abode, she was a friend of Marisol's. Not just any friend. Her best friend. Now there's something to add to my resume, I thought. I'm *shtupping* Miss Universe's best gal pal! As you can imagine, Paloma wasn't too shabby in the looks department herself. And though she was brashly uninhibited (I'd known her for all of twenty minutes when we'd had our get-right-to-it roof garden encounter), that was in no way a reflection upon her friend, as far as I could tell. Marisol struck me as being as sweet and wholesome as she appeared that night they placed the Miss Universe crown upon her head. When I met her she looked at me in a way that was reminiscent of how Julie Christie gazed searchingly into Warren Beatty's eyes in *Heaven Can Wait* and said, "You're the quarterback, aren't you?"

"Paloma has told me a lot about you," she said to me. Her eyes never let on as to what the deeper implications of that statement might have been.

# Chapter 48

## *BEAUTY AND THE BEAST*

I was sneaking past Luz, the receptionist at Channel 18, in my swim trunks and sandals—my jacket and tie in hand—when she said to hold it right there, Mr Brown! Hmmm...what did I do now? A rash of nasty phone calls had come in perhaps? Ah well, as long as my name was still on their lips…

"Only one call," she said. "Someone was asking about you."

"Hope it wasn't from the FBI," I said.

"Nope. It was a lady. Nydia Caro."

Hmmm...Nydia...I'd heard the name before. "Uh, she's a singer, no?"

"Yes, and I'm surprised you don't know more about her. You rate pretty big if she's interested in you."

In fact, I knew next to nothing about Nydia. I didn't know she was an up and coming Latin singing star (who has since become a legend) with her songs on all the Spanish stations.

"Anyway," Luz said, "I told her when you were normally here and she said she'd call back."

Some time passed, and indeed Nydia did call again. We had a convivial conversation, and I got invited to her home, no less, to meet her! Was I shocked? No. Pleasantly surprised, yes. But I had learned to expect the unexpected.

On the night of our meeting, I knocked on her door and her

roommate—who seemed to double as Nydia's secretary and chaperone—greeted me. I made myself comfortable on the sofa, chatted a while with the roommate, and waited for Nydia to make her grand entrance. A few minutes later she did, in a lovely white gown. There I was in a pair of jeans and some regular old shirt I had thrown on. Geez, I could have dressed up a little. But I was who I was. I hadn't yet caught onto the way most of the world worked—that to get what you wanted, you had to play the game.

Nydia Caro was—and remains to this day—one of the classic beauties. I've not included photos in this volume—you paint those mental pictures on your own—but there are tons of images out there in cyberspace that will be the proof of that pudding for you.

She asked me if I had been surprised at her calling me out of the blue. I said no, that women did that a lot with me. What an arrogant asshole I was! I could see the look of disappointment on her face. I didn't mean to lump her in with the ubiquitous groupies who always seemed to be around. But I could tell that's the way she took it.

We chatted for a while, and then I got the vibe that I should be excusing myself. Always leave 'em wanting more. She asked if she could give me a lift somewhere and I said sure, she could run me over to the Borinquen. I got into her Porsche and we rode through the night. There was still so much potential. A hand lightly placed upon my knee. Like when someone touches you on the shoulder as a way of showing they are interested. We talked about getting together sometime, and then we were there at my hotel. She gave me a tape of one of her songs to play on the radio. I played it, happy to help her promote her brand.

## CONJURING UP A GHOST...30 MINUTES BEFORE THE NEW YEAR

I was flipping around
and landed on one of the Spanish channels
and suddenly thought of you
and wondered what you'd be doing
about now
and wondering how your life turned out
minus me.

I didn't really know who you were
when you left that message
at the station
you wanted to meet me
that was how you operated
call and schedule an audience.

I didn't know your songs
were on the radio
or that you would sing
your national anthem
to a worldwide audience
the night George Foreman fought
that Puerto Rican kid
for the title in Tokyo.

I came over to your place
(took requests whenever possible)
and you made your grand entrance.

I knew you were disappointed
because I didn't dress up
and acted disinterested.

You drove me to the hotel
and I knew I had some balls
just asking you to do it.

Your roommate became the intermediary after that
and she said well, you are who you are
and she likes to go to the fancy clubs
and she's wondering
would you really be comfortable with that?

The last time I saw you was at the beach
you broke free from your entourage
came up and gave me a hug
and then you were gone.

You married one of your own
naturally
with little ones and that whole trip
and hell
don't know why
guess it's just that it's 30 minutes
till the new year
and those bikini waxed babes are
shakin' and grinding their asses up on the screen
would Dick Clark approve?
(oh well, he's dead)
I used to think that was something
but now it just grosses me out
we both came from a time and a place
when women had more class
and a lot more grace.

I checked you out on YouTube
and yes you're still a beauty
though time takes its toll
and the glitter wears off
and so I'm wondering
did your fame bring you happiness
you know 'cause
it all ends up in the same place

in the end
and maybe you're thinking it too
sitting here
30 minutes till the new year
recalling that old Peggy Lee song
Is That All There Is?

    The movies are full of fairy-tale stories of how opposites attract and live happily ever after. But the reality is that casual guys and fancy ladies don't mix. She was out of my league. But I'll always hold a soft spot for her here in my oft-trampled upon heart.

# Chapter 49

## *TO THE MOON, ALICE!*

I've often said of my generation that we were pioneers in space exploration. But that was inner, not outer space. These puny steps we've made to explore the physical cosmos pale in comparison to the way that Timothy Leary, Ram Dass, and Alan Watts—to name some of my favorites—guided us on our journey of exploration through the universe of expanded consciousness. That said, the first moon landing—which took place on July 20th, 1969—was still a big deal. It showed us, as physical beings, what we were capable of besides hate, war, and callous disregard for the well-being of our host planet.

The lunar landing was televised live, and for those who couldn't be near their sets, WBMJ aired the audio as it occurred as well. I was at the helm in the control room, I threw it to newsman John Simon, who said a few introductory words, and then we joined the network feed. All on the edge of our seats as this most momentous occasion in the history of mankind was about to play itself out. As Neil Armstrong was descending the ladder to take his first steps onto the lunar surface...everything went silent. *We had lost the network feed!* Simon, in the newsroom, began cursing. I waved my arms frantically to get his attention because he had inadvertently left his microphone on, and everything that was spewing out of his mouth was going out live to our listening audience.

We got the audio feed restored after a short while, but there may still be a few folks who were listening to us that night who think that Neil Armstrong's first words for all posterity were: SHIT! GODDAMNIT!

# Chapter 50

## LOTTA FREAKS!

The *Mar Y Sol Pop* Festival took place in early April, 1972, at a beachside location in Manati, Puerto Rico, about 30 miles from San Juan. It has largely lapsed into obscurity in the annals of rock music history. There was bad publicity due to some accidental deaths at the beach, and a young person getting fatally stabbed inside his tent. That aside, *Mar Y Sol* had everything a typical festival goer could want. Big name bands, drugs, and folks coming from near and far to frolic in their birthday suits and get back to the garden. Some of the major names that performed were: Allman Brothers, Alice Cooper, Dave Brubeck, Emerson, Lake and Palmer, Faces (with Rod Stewart), Billy Joel, B.B. King, and The J. Geils Band.

    WBMJ was helping to promote the festival. I don't remember how much of that was paid advertising (if any) and how much was the word of mouth that we jocks were encouraged to spill into the wind by a Mr. Bill Dial, who was handling some of the local promotion for the festival. Dial was a bearish guy who'd often show up at the station in bib overalls (because bib overalls are the standard uniform for bearish guys). If the name is at all familiar to you, Bill Dial would go on a few years later to write several episodes of the hit network TV show, *WKRP In Cincinnati*—

which was a delightfully accurate portrayal of the kind of characters you'll meet and what actually goes on inside a radio station!

Bill would stop in now and then to get us up to speed on how preparations for the festival were going. At some point he and I discussed the idea of having me introduce one of the acts on stage. I could bring on Emerson, Lake and Palmer, he thought. He told me to just go around to the back of the stage when I got there and ask for him, and he would set it up. Well, that settled it. I would be going to the festival with bells and bell bottoms on. I was looking forward to it. Then again, I didn't have anyone to go with. That problem was settled when two cute brunettes—Catalina and Josie—showed up at the station and mentioned that they would be attending, and would I like to come along with them? I graciously accepted their offer, since it meant I wouldn't have to drive and I'd have two (for the price of one) lovelies to hang out with.

We passed a joint around in the car on the way over to Manati, to ensure that our heads would be in fine fettle when we got there. The first thing I remember noticing upon arrival at the festival grounds was a rather portly young woman soaping herself in the buff at one of the open-air communal shower stalls. Here and there a naked person would be walking alongside a fully clothed person and neither seemed out of place. This was *freedom*, man!

The sweet smell of Mary Jane permeated the air as Catalina, Josie and I made our way toward the main stage area. We picked our way through the sea of bodies and found a spot reasonably close to the stage. We spread our blanket onto the ground and settled in, with me all cozy and snug between the two of them. We lit up another doobie to make sure we'd be right in tune with the mellow vibe. My head was screwed on, but it wasn't straight! A little ways away at the beach, young folks were testing the waters in various stages of undress. The nudity was one thing. There was an innocence about it. That's why the state of undress is referred to as being *au naturel*. The natural state of being. Public sex, on the other hand, would be greatly frowned upon in this kind of setting.

We were about to violate that taboo.

I don't remember who made the first move, but suddenly Josie and I were all over each other. Our mouths locked in a passionate soul kiss. Her fingers moved teasingly along my inner thigh. She fumbled insistently with the button on my jeans and loosened it. She slid her hand down my pants. She got a grip on things. She tugged at my zipper. She freed my Willie into the open air as if he were in need of soaking up some rays. Should we be doing this, I thought, with all these folks crowded around us? Was I going to tell her to stop? I reciprocated by sliding my hand inside her short shorts to feel her wetness. Our passionate soul kiss continued the whole time without letting up. We were multi-tasking. Music blared from the stage but I didn't take note of who was performing. Josie's nimble fingers were playing a sweeter tune on my instrument.

It occurred to me that people might be watching us. I mean here was a girl blatantly wanking a guy in the middle of a crowd, so somebody was going to notice. I felt embarrassed at the thought. But Benjamin Franklin said, "Idle hands are the devil's playthings." He couldn't have foreseen all the interpretations of that. The exquisite feelings engendered by Josie's diligent efforts became overwhelming. She wasn't going to stop until she felt something warm and wet on her fingers. I rewarded her determination by shooting off in her fist. The answer to the question of whether we were being observed came quickly, as I heard someone behind us exclaim: *Goddamn!* Yes...goddamn...as in: *Hoo boy...we didn't know all this would be included in the price of admission!* As for Catalina, she never moved from her spot—either trying to pretend she didn't know us, or observing the whole thing out of the corner of her eye. She just kept smiling. She was a cool chick.

Josie and I came to our senses shortly thereafter and tried to make ourselves look presentable again. It was just one of those things, as Cole Porter would have said. Then I remembered that I was supposed to report backstage! It was getting dark, and I didn't know what the hell was going on. I made my way erratically toward the stage area, trying to make sure that my shirt was covering up the wet stain on the front of my jeans.

At the rear of the stage I got some guy's attention. "Hi, man," I said. "Is Bill Dial around?"

"No, man," he said. "Bill ain't here."

"Uh...you know when he'll be back?"

"Don't know, man."

"Er...okay, man. Later."

I headed back to find my two nubile companions. Wasn't anything a big deal, man. Wasn't anything a big deal. The night was young. Anything could yet happen. And there was music in the air.

# Chapter 51

## *THE TIMES THEY WERE A CHANGIN'*

99 percent of all popular songwriters were hopeless romantics who "couldn't live without" some particular person. Is it any wonder that we all grew up so needy? That began to change in the mid sixties when songwriters began to have more of a social conscience, and the protest song came into its own. There were many great writers who contributed to the movement—led, of course, by Mr Bob Dylan. Barry McGuire summed up the turbulent state of the world with "Eve Of Destruction." And there was no song that flew in the face of those who ran the war machine better than Country Joe McDonald's "Fixin' To Die Rag" as it was performed at Woodstock. It asked the fundamental question: *What are we fighting for?* The tragedy of Vietnam was that beyond the jingoistic rhetoric and the bogus "domino theory," nobody really knew. The song that still resonates so strongly today, because it contains the ultimate truth of why we fight, is Buffy Saint Marie's "Universal Soldier." Personal responsibility. So many unquestioningly gave their bodies as a weapon of the war.

We live in a world where the tail wags the dog. It has always been that way, perhaps due to some hive mentality (all hail The Queen) inherent in the human race and insects alike...the few dictate to the many. A handful of policy makers decide what's going down, and all along the chain of command the orders are carried out and set into action by whoever gives the final directive to deploy troops from one global hotspot to another, for example. Buffy Saint Marie was trying to wake us to the reality that those barking out the commands have *zero* power to enforce them unless the rest of us go along in lockstep. *Just following orders.* (And asking do you want fries with that?) Down through history, and up to the present day, the poignant words of The Kingston Trio still echo: *When will we ever learn?*

# Chapter 52

## *DOOMSDAY IN DALLAS*

I belong to an exclusive fraternity. Those men and women who were on the air at TV and radio stations across the land when the bulletin came down that there had been an attempt on the life of President John F. Kennedy. It fell upon us to interrupt whatever program was running and deliver the news to a shocked and horrified nation. Maybe you only saw Walter Cronkite. But there were many of us on a local level who especially will never forget where they were on that day, each with his own personal story.

November 22nd, 1963. It was my first job in radio at a station in the midwest. It was a Saturday, and there was nobody else in the building, as those who pulled weekend shifts typically ran the whole operation by themselves. The first bulletin came across on the UPI newswire—it was a teletype machine that went clackety-clack. It was a comforting sound. It assured you that something was happening somewhere in the world, and it wasn't "fake news." Journalists in those days took their responsibility seriously. They were committed to a just-the-facts-ma'am kind of impartiality. They weren't going to slant or distort the news. They weren't paid shills for some political agenda.

The first bulletin came out garbled, as if someone was typing with flying fingers just to get it out there. But I could make out the gist of it. I dashed back to the control room, opened the mic and delivered the terse statement. An attempt had been made on the life of the president. I assured my listeners that they would be the first to know of further developments. And now, back to music. There was an anxious time period when we were waiting to hear if the president may have survived. I heard the machine start up again and I ran down the hall to grab the next bulletin (also garbled). I sprinted back to the control room, took a deep breath, and turned on the mic. In a very stoic and emotionless tone, I announced that the president was dead.

I don't remember feeling anything. I was numb. I loved JFK, but it was part of my survival mechanism going back to the early teenage years to numb out. So I didn't cry. I never cried. I was an eighteen year-old kid, faking my way through it.

The importance of that as a survival skill cannot be minimized.

# Chapter 53

## *LOVE IS ALL YOU NEED*

In Puerto Rico we were taking our cues from trends that were happening in the states. The "Love-In" became a thing. What was a Love-In? It was a happening, man. What was a happening? Something that happens.

The times they were indeed a changing. But some found it hard to keep up as they nursed their old ideas about morality from previous decades. There was a Love-In at one of the big parks. I saw this girl I knew—Casey—who was wearing a crochet mesh top with no bra underneath. Her pert nipples were peeping right through there in a *howdy pardner* kind of way! Some officers of the law came along, and doing their duty to protect the public from such dangers to society (remember Lana and her "inappropriate" bikini?), they told Casey she couldn't be running loose like that in public, and that she would either have to leave or change into something more appropriate. No problem. She pulled the mesh top up over her head and freed her breasts (and they were spectacular!). She stood there nonchalantly, topless in front of the officers—which sure did seem counterproductive to what they were trying to accomplish—while she rummaged around in her bag to come up with a replacement top that would meet with the officers' approval. I had dropped some acid before coming to the park, and it was kicking in pretty good at that point. Boy, did that little episode with the intimidating titties seem funny!

There was music playing and it was reverberating and phase-shifting inside my head. The beautiful folks in their colorful attire were milling about and strolling through the park—sending out love vibes. As I looked at them, they all turned into giant cockroaches walking upright! You can say it was a hallucination, but I prefer to think it was one of those moments of cosmic illumination. I understood that we were all cockroaches in some other being's world...and all gods in someone else's. From that moment on I began to meditate on the meaning of the word *compassion*.

# Chapter 54

## *THEY GOT SOME CRAZY LITTLE WOMEN THERE*

My colleague Scott Brady from WBMJ (he'd sometimes call himself "Sweet" Scott Brady, but he wasn't sweet in that way) was an active duty member of the U.S. Navy, stationed at the Sabana Seca base not far from our studios. He was doing some part-time work for us when he was off duty. He was allowed to live off base and took advantage of that opportunity by becoming my roommate at my pad at the Miramar Towers. We were good buddies and it was a good fit. He would entertain his "guests" in his room, and I would entertain mine at the other end of the apartment down the hall.

Brady was a funny guy. He "loved" the navy so much that he had a calendar on his bedroom wall where he was counting down the days until his hitch was up. He had what was to be his last day in the service circled and he'd written in large letters: OUT...OUT...OUT OF THE FUCKING NAVY!!!

The seagoing branch of the U.S. military had been no friend to Puerto Rico. They'd been using the neighboring inhabited island of Vieques for bombing runs and target practice (for over sixty years in total until operations were shut down in 2001). It created a health and environmental crisis for the island and its approximately nine thousand inhabitants. The navy used agent orange and other toxic chemicals during the course of its operations on Vieques. The Department of Health issued a study indicating that the incidence of cancer among the island's population was significantly higher than the rest of Puerto Rico. I'm only touching on it here—the information is readily available out there for anyone who cares to learn the whole shameful story. It could have been another reason why Brady wanted out. He was a good guy, and I'm sure he didn't care to be looked upon as a symbol of the government's callous disregard for the health and safety of its own people. You could say he led a double life between the military and civilian worlds, as I led a double life as Charlie Brown and "Not Charlie Brown" (according to some people!).

*

I entered the pool area at the Borinquen one early evening to find that the bar was doing a brisk business. All the stools were occupied, which was a bit unusual. Then I saw that there was one person in the middle of it all—holding forth—as the expression goes. He was a stout looking middle-aged guy, and there was something very familiar about that face. Didn't take long for me to catch on that it was ALDO RAY—noted film actor whose heyday was in the fifties. Ray was best known for his tough guy roles in war movies—*Battle Cry* (1955) being his most successful box office hit. He worked with all of the legends—Humphrey Bogart, Spencer Tracy, Rita Hayworth, Katherine Hepburn and on down the line. Ray had chosen our beloved Borinquen to hang out at and regale those who had gathered round with his personal reflections and remembrances of his life and times and some of those stars (the temperamental ones always elicited the most oohs and ahhs!).

There was this gal named Sandy. Nicest woman you'd ever want to meet. But when she got drunk she had this habit of trying to stick her hand down the nearest guy's pants, and she didn't care where she was. She would come up to me and it would be like hi...how ya doin...and she'd stick her hand right down the front of my jeans! I'd be trying to listen to Aldo Ray and discourage Sandy from doing this thing in public (very distracting) of which she would have no recollection of when she sobered up, which ensured that the behavior would be repeated indefinitely. Mr Ray would be holding forth nightly at the pool bar, and Sandy would be floating through the crowd like a pickpocket looking for her next unsuspecting target. I could see that under the right circumstances, though, she would be one you might like to have around.

Couldn't say the same for our Exhibit B. Yvonne was her name and I would run into her from time to time. She claimed to have taken all the Lebron Brothers on at once (how many were there?) and being the kind of girl she was, I took her at her word. Scott Brady and I had entered the elevator and were heading up to Penthouse One. She ducked in there just before the doors closed. I don't know where she thought she was going. She wasn't with us. There was a conservative looking family of three who were also along for the ride—mom, dad, and their wholesome corn-fed daughter of about thirteen. Probably from the midwest. It was quiet as a jukebox at 5am in there when Yvonne blurted out: LET GO OF MY TIT, CHARLIE BROWN!

I wasn't touching her.

I was mortified. Yvonne was a skank who had zero class, and this was her idea of pulling a funny. I felt so embarrassed for this family, who must have discarded the idea of any further trips to the island right then and there. But I was an easy target for those kind of cheap shots. It went with the territory. (By the way, there were five Lebron brothers.)

Delving further into the realm of cheap shots. There was this semi-acquaintance of mine—a guy I'd see around the bar sometimes—and one night I overheard him making snarky remarks about my performance on channel 18 to one of his friends. He knew I was there and that I was within earshot of him. But it was okay. I let it slide off my back.

As it happened, one of my young friends named George came to me shortly thereafter and asked me for a favor. He had reserved a room at the hotel for a clandestine rendezvous he'd set up with a girl, but something had come up last minute and he wouldn't be able to make the appointment. He had no way to get a hold of her, so he asked if I could be there waiting in the room when she arrived to deliver his heartfelt apology. I agreed to do it. No problem.

I knew that whoever showed up wasn't going there to play Chinese checkers with George. She was looking for some action.

Sooo...when I got to the room I removed my pants and waited for her to show. The knock on the door came and I welcomed her inside. Holy smokes...I recognized her as the girlfriend of the snarky critic of mine from the bar! She was a pouty little Puerto Rican witch, but sexy in that witchy kind of way. And I could see why she was there, as her boyfriend was no prized pig.

She looked at me warily. "Where's George?" she asked.

"George couldn't make it," I said. "He asked me to tell you that he's really sorry."

She looked down and saw that I did not have a matching pair of trousers to go with my shirt. "You've got no pants on!" she said. "Put some pants on."

"Well, instead of that...I've got a better idea. Why don't *you* take your dress off?"

"You want me to take my dress off?"

"Uh...think that's what I said."

She thought about it for like, three seconds, and then the dress came off! She wasn't going to waste the opportunity just because George wasn't there, and I dare say I was an upgrade from my friend anyway.

It occurs to me that I may be giving the impression that all the women back then would hop into bed with you at the drop of a hat. That wasn't true. Some would. Actually, a lot of them would. But not all of them would. I hope that clears it up once and for all.

I did that girl every which way but loose, and she was down

for every bit of it. It made me happy because I would forever have one up on her boyfriend, and he would be clueless about it. But when we were finished, she had the *audacity* to start nitpicking little things about my technique. I couldn't believe it. Everybody's a critic! If this were the Sexual Olympics, she would have been the nasty Russian judge who consistently gives out lower marks than all the others. She and her now cuckolded beau belonged together.

At least she didn't say *incorrigible incompetence!*

# Chapter 55

## *A LOVE THAT SHINES*

I was strolling along the beach—grooving on the sun, the sand, the bikinis. I took note of a young woman lying there, all greased up like the bottom of a pie tin and baking to a golden brown in the sun. She had this blonde surfer girl look going on. She was worthy of another look, I thought. I walked a little farther down the beach and then turned around to make another pass and check her out again, whistling some inane tune. On the return she caught me by surprise when she sat up and said, "Hello, Mister Brown!" Shit, my cover was blown. I still wasn't used to being recognized. Guess she'd been watching channel 18.

 Her name was Lisa. She was one of the more recent arrivals from the mainland who were giving the island a shot to win them over and become a place they could call home. Cut to the chase. We went out and got really cozy with each other that first night. I didn't call her the next day. Dating etiquette dictated that you put a little space between that first and second contact. So you didn't appear too anxious. Too needy. Too hot on her tail. Too much like a lapdog with his tongue dangling obscenely from his drooling mouth. So I waited a day and then went over and knocked on her door. She was living with a girlfriend—Miki—the person who had lured her to the island in the first place.

 She asked me why I had waited so long! She thought that

maybe I wasn't coming back. We sat there across from each other, and then something remarkable happened. My gaze was locked on hers. Her gaze was locked on mine. I could see something shining in her eyes. I'm not speaking figuratively. This was an actual thing they call the *love-light*. Gleaming. Gleaming in her eyes! We couldn't tear our gaze away from each other. Then the brightest smile illuminated her face and she laughed.

"What is HAPPENING?" she said.

I wasn't going to pretend. "You know," I said.

"Yes...I do," she said.

We were falling in love right then and there!

*

Lisa had multiple sclerosis. It was as shitty of a hand as life could deal to a beautiful person in her mid-twenties. The disease affected her gait to the point of where she could easily be mistaken for a late night drunk meandering along, but she didn't let it stop her. There was a guy who had been a professional masseur who would come over and give her leg and thigh massages on a regular basis. She said those helped a lot. I started sitting in to observe his technique, so I could fill in and do the massages for her when he wasn't around. It took me a while, but I gradually got better at it, and Lisa seemed appreciative of my efforts.

She was smart and funny. Did I tell you how important it is to be close to someone with a wicked sense of humor? It's everything. You think comedians do what they do just as a fun way to make a living? Hardly. They do it for survival. What was always in the back of Lisa's mind was that MS might someday put her into a wheelchair. But we didn't dwell on that. The MS was a thing, but it wasn't the thing that defined our relationship. We talked, jokingly at first, of getting married. I remember the day when we brought up the subject. It was just a whimsical what-if at that point, but when we jumped into a cab to return from the beach, she blurted out: We're getting married!! to the driver. We accepted his congratulations, each of us grinning from ear to ear and we weren't even stoned.

*

Sometimes I would stay over at Lisa's place, and sometimes she would stay at mine.

The nice upscale apartment building—the Miramar Towers—where I had recently taken up residence was just a stone's throw from the Borinquen Hotel and the radio station. Great neighborhood.

Lisa and I were walking along the tree-lined streets one lovely evening, just to get some air and some exercise. We were no more than a block away from my building, when a car pulled up, not stopping directly beside us but a few yards down the street. Someone called out from the vehicle, asking in Spanish if we had any matches. "No *fumar!*" Lisa shot back at them. We started to resume our walk, no doubt looking like a couple of tipsy American tourists, considering Lisa's swaying-in the-breeze manner of motating. Two young guys got out of the car and sprinted over to us. I thought maybe they didn't understand what we were telling them...

The one guy, whom I never got a decent look at, grabbed ahold of my arm and stuck the sharp blade of a knife flush against the flesh of my neck. Just like that, and we hadn't been properly introduced! His partner—I only remember that he had dark curly hair and was a nice looking chap—stood two feet directly in front of me and pointed the barrel of his revolver at the space between my eyes. "Alright...this is a holdup!" he announced.

I was incredulous..."You've got to be kidding!" I said. How was this happening? In this neighborhood?

He shook his head. "May I have your wallet, please?"

At least he was polite. That made me feel a little better, but not much. By the way, I suggest if you ever find yourself in a similar situation, the best thing to do is cooperate. Don't try to be a hero. Especially if a loved one is with you and could suffer the consequences of a situation that goes terribly awry. Unless they want you to get into a vehicle with them. Then you gotta fight like hell.

I handed over my wallet and the gunman opened it with one hand (he must have had practice) while keeping his weapon trained on me. Which was scarier? It was the cold steel of the knife blade pressing against my flesh. One wrong move and...

The gunman took a moment to count the loot. I had a hundred and twenty bucks in there, all in twenties. I normally carried a bit of cash—perhaps for just such an unforeseen expenditure as this! In retrospect it was good that I did. His partner said something about checking Lisa.

"She doesn't have anything!" I said. I didn't want them touching her.

The gunman finished counting. He was satisfied with the take. He courteously handed my wallet back to me. "Let's go!" he said to his accomplice. They took off and hopped back into their car, pulling away slowly with the lights off.

"Are you all right?" I asked Lisa.

"Yeah," she said. "What about you?

"I'm all right, but I think our strolling days in this neighborhood are over."

I had meandered through the darkened streets and alleyways of Old San Juan late at night and nothing remotely like this had ever happened. But maybe things were changing, and this was the new face of entrepreneurship on the island. These enterprising young lads had developed their own way of cashing in on the tourist trade, or at least what they perceived to be so. Tourists were going to be there for a week—two weeks tops. They weren't going to want to get involved in a lengthy police investigation that would likely lead nowhere to begin with. So most of them weren't going to report it.

Brilliant.

*

I was staying over at Lisa's place—the one she shared with Miki, her housemate. I'd administered Lisa's leg massages and we had turned in for the night. It was about 2am when I rolled over to find an empty space on the other side of the bed. Maybe she had just gone to the crapper. Some time passed and she still hadn't returned. I got up and tippy-toed through the darkened house. Miki would sometimes have other houseguests who would stay over, and on this night a friend of hers—Antoine—was there. When I got to the living room I reeled back in shock. I didn't know what to make of it. There was Lisa sitting upright at one end of the sofa. Antoine—a pretty boy with hair down to there—was stretched out along the length of the couch with his head cradled in her lap. And oh yeah...he was naked from the waist down. I said something sarcastic like oh, don't let me interrupt you two, and headed back to the bedroom to find my clothes. Lisa jumped up and said, "No, honey...we're not doing anything! Antoine is depressed and I'm just trying to comfort him a little because he's, like...he's really *depressed*..." Antoine backed up her profession of innocence.

Nonetheless I headed back to the bedroom with Lisa following and telling me not to be so silly.

"The guy has no pants on!" I said.

"So?"

"A dangling dick is the trunk of the elephant in the room!"

"Oh, come on,'" she said. "I didn't even notice. I was only trying to help soothe his pain."

Now, you must keep in mind that there was more nudity in

those days, and most people chalked it up to young folks just expressing their free-spiritedness (nice old landladies and officers of the law notwithstanding) and let it go at that. So, trying to make my most liberal interpretation of the situation...there was still something that didn't seem quite right, Call me old fashioned, I guess.

I put my clothes on and told Lisa I didn't think I'd be able to get back to sleep, and I would just get an early start and head back to my place. She really didn't understand why I was acting like a poophead. I pouted for a couple days. She was apologetic. Then I let it go because I wanted to give her the benefit of the doubt. (I told you that was my biggest flaw, didn't I?)

Hey, what do YOU think, pardner? Write to me. Call me! Because to this day it's one of those things I go back and forth in my addled brain about.

*

Lisa came to me with what to her was exciting news. There was a doctor who was developing some "revolutionary" therapies for MS. The down side of it was that he was in Germany. Where she had heard about this man I didn't know. She was elated, though, because it offered her some hope that maybe this thing could be turned around. She would, of course, investigate it further.

Some time went by, and we went on doing the things that we did. Laughing...making love...sometimes going out to dinner or for drinks where I could show her off. (She cleaned up well.)

Then one day she told me that she had been in touch with the doctor in Germany, and that he had agreed to take her on as a project. I was happy for her, but my heart was sinking. She would be leaving for Germany in a few weeks.

The days leading up to her departure went by like a hazy dream sequence in a movie. What could I say to her? Don't go? You don't tell a person who is being swept down a river not to grasp for tree roots or anything along the bank that might save her. Even if she's only clutching at straws. She didn't know how long she'd be over there. It all depended, of course, on how things went. But she'd be back. Of course, she'd be back!

The morning she left there was a hazy blue-grey sky. Miki was taking her to the airport. Lisa preferred it that way. Goodbyes are so stupid. You want to say this...you want to say that...in the end you say not that much because you need to keep your brave face on. Lisa gazed back at me as Miki's car pulled slowly away.

Somehow I knew that it was the last time I would see her.

# Chapter 56

*1973*

Gas was 40 cents a gallon.

The World Trade Center in New York City became the world's tallest building.

*Roe v. Wade* made abortion a constitutional right.

Congress established the *Endangered Species Act*.

Monica Lewinski was born.

The Partridge Family was one of our most popular television shows.

At the movie theaters, The Exorcist was scaring the shit out of everybody, including me.

Secretariat won the Triple Crown.

Richard Nixon was sworn in for his second term as president.

The Watergate scandal erupted.

The Vietnam War came to a close.

And with it "the sixties" were symbolically fading as well. The war had galvanized an entire generation. A generation that believed it could change the world. And for a time, in fact, it did.

And while I had no sense of it as another digit was added to our cumulative illusion of time, my tenure on the island had nearly run its course as well. And I still hadn't found lasting love. The tragedy of that being that if a nice guy...or a bastard (cast your votes NOW) such as myself couldn't find true love in a tropical paradise, where would he find it? Was love just an illusion like everything else?

My life had been about overcoming adversity. The Comeback Kid. But love may be the toughest opponent of all, especially when it knocks you down for an eight count, and you have to make the decision to get back up again and get right back in the fray. We can't allow disappointment in love, or anything else that goes down in this life, to turn us into emotional pillars of salt. You have to just go for it. You've got to be all in every time. You have to welcome pain like an old friend who stopped by that you can entertain for a while, but if he wants to stay too long, you've got to give him his walking papers and kick his ass to the curb. And make him take his baggage with him. It's the only way we can start anew with a clean slate and a clear eye, ready to put it all on the line once again. Once you understand that it's not about avoiding pain, but absorbing it and fighting on, you are free. This is how we approach the game of life if we want to have no regrets on the way out of the stadium (even if there's a riot going on around you!), regardless of the final score.

# Chapter 57

## *RADIO ROCK*

It came down like this. One day they called the air staff in and informed us that there would be some "changes" made. WBMJ was going to employ native Spanish speakers as its deejays, and change the moniker of the station to *Radio Rock*. The reasons given us as to why the switch was being made were kept vague. Bob Bennett, for all that he was, was first and foremost a management type. He was practiced in the art of keeping an air staff guessing as to why anything was being done, at the direction of ownership. "We're moving in a new direction" was a universally used cop-out phrase employed throughout the industry when booting someone out on his ass. (As common as "We're sorry for your loss" was on all of the TV cop shows.)

One had to assume that a big part of it was wanting to communicate more effectively with the island's predominantly Spanish speaking population. None of us gringos on the staff were fluent in the language (should have paid more attention in those Berlitz classes—damn!) But it would all feed into the fact that the bottom line is at the heart of everything in radio—and that indicated that the move was being made to address some pressing financial concerns.

Privately, Bob Bennett told me that there was still some discussion going on as to whether I might be retained, being the most recognizable and still beloved (I assumed) of the air personalities. But shortly thereafter I learned that no, the powers that be wanted to make it a clean sweep. Out with the new and in with the old, if you get my drift. Thus the countdown as to how I would spend the rest of my days on this earth had begun. The channel 18 thing was a part-time gig and wouldn't be enough to sustain me long term. I briefly thought about WHOA, but discarded that idea when I remembered I was on Sally Jessy's "Do Not Send Christmas Card" list. And that brand of radio would have required me to tone my boisterous instincts down to cater to their "adult" audience. I couldn't imagine anything more stultifying.

The writing was on the wall. The process that had brought me to the island—getting those audition tapes and resumes circulating out there—would now begin anew. I was headed back to the mainland. I silently thanked the good people of Puerto Rico for taking me into their hearts. There would be other cities and towns and other radio stations "up and down the dial." But there would never be another ride like this one, and I knew it.

# Chapter 58

## *ROLL UP FOR THE MYSTERY TOUR*

Nothing is permanent. Any Buddhist will tell you that. And God was lonely being the BIG CHEESE as a solo act, so he divided himself into all the myriad Lego pieces—the animal, mineral, and vegetable kingdoms—every galaxy in the heavens and every grain of sand...every you and every me... just for the cosmically orgasmic experience of getting it on with an "other." Any Hindu will tell you that. But I don't prescribe to religious belief systems. I have a system for playing the horses that I follow religiously. There's a lot of faith involved in that too. I've been to the mountaintop. And I've seen—like *Siddhartha* saw...like *Sai Baba* saw...like *Paramahansa Yogananda* saw...like *John Lennon* saw...that we all shine on. It's enough to know. If there were no mystery surrounding the whole she-bang, the Wizard Of Oz would still be playing with himself behind that curtain, waiting for those motley misfits—who were never going to show—to seek him out.

If there's any legitimate knock on my generation, it's that we saw a direct route to arrive at these truths and we took it, when we could have and should have delved more into the natural highs—yoga, meditation—that sort of thing. Same end result but without many of the nasty side effects. But we all possessed a kind of innocence about it, and because of that there were excesses. They had names like Jimi, Janis, and Jim. We were pioneers in space exploration, if you will, and the lessons learned should have been a red flag to succeeding generations to slow down and move with caution. (Advice from elders is generally ignored.)

    That said, if I had a time machine, I'd go back there in a New York nanosecond. Believing once again that Love, and only Love, is the driving force in the universe.

# Chapter 59

## *TIME WARP IN AISLE #5*

Moving down the aisle at the
SuperDuper market, a song from
1968 comes on the overhead speakers:
*Hi everybody, I'm Archie Bell of The Drells
from Houston Texas...*

just as if none of this crazy shit
had taken place in the interim and we
are back to the purity of The Beat.

*We don't only sing, but we dance
just as good as we want*
just as if this 3 ring circus
hadn't come to town to stay,
and we realized too late we'd
given the ringmaster too much
discretion and now he's wading
into the crowd with the whip
once reserved only for the lions.

But this message from on high
that's washing me in the blood
is as primal as a heartbeat
and the old gal with her cart
that's doubling as a walker
is moving her hips in a way
that tells me to look away

I'VE GOT ANTS IN MY PANTS
LET'S DANCE!

And whether all of this bullshit
falls away one day
or we're in for a dystopian future
that'll make 1984 seem like
a mere prologue, my permanent escape

through the time warp in aisle # 5
is already booked,
knowing that all must pass
'cept for the one and only thing
that will save us in the end...
THE BEAT!!!

# Chapter 60

## *OH, ONE LAST THING*

As my days at WBMJ were dwindling down to a precious few, I received a knock-me-over-with-a-feather surprise. I picked up the phone to hear a familiar voice, ghostlike through the eerie long distance line noise.

It was *Ally*.

She was on the mainland. I forgot about everything that had gone down before and just warmed to the sound of her voice. We spoke in that gentle way of two people who had had time to reflect upon the past and arrive at a more forgiving space. I gave her the lowdown of all the changes that were taking place and that I was soon expecting to find myself stateside as well. Cut to the chase: we agreed to meet up. Ostensibly as friends, to see where it might lead. I told her I was planning to stop and visit the people who had raised me at their farm in Iowa before I did anything else. She said she had no problem meeting me someplace nearby. So it was set. I would take her out to the farm, smack dab in the middle of the Corn and Bible Belt, to meet some simple, down to earth folk. I wondered WHAT they would truly think of Ally.

That, my friend, is a whole other story!

# Acknowledgments

Many thanks and a debt of gratitude to my editor, OJ Modjeska, who planted the seed of this book in my brain.

With fond remembrance of my high school English instructor, Lloyd Oakley McDole, who slipped up by inadvertently laughing at one of my subversive poems, and by doing so pointed the way to my future..

And special recognition to all those who touched me in some uniquely persona way, including:

Henry Miller, Andrew Marvell, John Fowles, Will Elder, Frank Zappa, Marlon Brando, Wolfman Jack, Dick Biondi, Jim Morrison, The Ronettes, Herb Graham, Alan Watts, Rocky Balboa, The French Impressionists, and last but not least Brigitte Bardot, who inspired me to want to grow into an adult...even though I never quite made it that far.

www.ingramcontent.com/pod-product-compliance
Lightning Source LLC
Chambersburg PA
CBHW031443040426
42444CB00007B/944